DESTINY *Helper*

PROPHET SAM OLU-ALO
©2021

ISBN: 978-978-986-853-7

Published by
Cgnature Creativemedia Ltd.
t: +234.708.684.2032
t: +234.812 365 5747
e: cgnaturestudio@gmail.com

*All scripture quotations are from the King James Version
of the Bible, except otherwise stated.*

*This book is dedicated to the glory of God,
my family and the entire Glorious Generation
Partners (Home & Abroad).*

ACKNOWLEDGEMENT

All thanks be to God the giver of all wisdom, the author and finisher of my faith, for truly I am who I am in Him who loved me and gave Himself, so I can partake of His everlasting grace and mercy. I also honour all my Fathers in the Lord in the Christ Apostolic Church (CAC) Worldwide.

I must also thank my darling wife - Oluwayemisi for her tireless support towards the work of ministry and our lovely children Oore-ofe, Inioluwa and Oluwatosimile.

I must not fail to acknowledge the Chairman of my Glorious Generation Partners (Home & Abroad) - Mr. Ade Olabode, our various coordinators in US, Canada, UK/EU, Nigeria and everyone of you my Partners who continue to inspire me and support our work of ministry.

To my publishers, editorial team, in particular, Mrs. Yetunde Elebunibon and Mr. Afolabi Imoukhuede, thank you all for the painstaking work, and the many sleepless nights to push out this work in record time.

To all my readers, may you found helpers that would push forward your destiny, Amen.

Prophet Sam Olu-Alo
February 2021

CONTENTS

Acknowledgement   *v*
Foreword   *xi*

CHAPTER 1
What is Destiny?
13

CHAPTER 2
Destiny Helper
23

CHAPTER 3
Why You Must Fulfil Destiny
33

CHAPTER 4
Destiny Helpers You Need in Your Life
49

CHAPTER 5
What to Do to Ensure You Meet
with Your Destiny Helper
73

CHAPTER 6

Hindrances or Obstacles that Can Deny
You of Your Destiny Helpers
81

CHAPTER 7

Why Destiny Helpers Refuse to Help
91

CHAPTER 8

How to Sustain Destiny Helper
97

ADDENDUM

Important Notes/ Prayers for Destiny Carriers
when Faced with Challenges
105

FOREWORD

This book titled, "Destiny Helper" written by renown Prophet Olu-Alo, who is a child of God and a highly anointed man of God. He is a preacher of the gospel of Jesus Christ. He is a reputable and international minister of God who has written a book of this magnitude as inspired by God.

This book is timely and God moved to deliver the readers from bondage of destiny snatchers and killers as written from biblical perspective with prayer points that are accessible to the readers that will turn situations around in their favour by God. This eight, rather nine-chaptered book, was written by this highly anointed and reputable man of God. Although, originally written as a eight-chaptered book, but as I go through it critically, I see the addendum as an additional chapter.

The author, Prophet Olu-Alu, presents Chapters One and Two to define, from biblical perspective, destiny and destiny helper; Chapter Three entrenches rationale for destiny fulfilment;

Chapter Four presents helpers needed in life; while Chapter Five talks more on your obligations before you are connected to your destiny helpers; Chapter Six advances hindrances and obstacles that robs an individual of destiny helpers; Chapter Seven clearly spells out reasons why destiny helpers may refuse to help; Chapter Eight discusses strategies for sustaining destiny helpers and an addendum that I perceived as Chapter Nine is prayerfully packaged on how to overcome challenges that may raise their ugly heads against destiny carriers.

I therefore have no hesitation, rather enthusiastic, to recommend this philosophical, psychological, biblical, ministerial and spiritual book by this reputable and anointed man of God, Prophet, Pastor and Evangelist Olu-Alo to the readers who are thirsty to fulfil their destinies.

Pastor/Associate Professor Abayomi, A.A.
The Coordinator,
CACTS, BSPE, Ilesa.
February 2021

CHAPTER 1

What is Destiny?

*And the Lord God said, It is not good that the man should be
alone; I will make him an help meet for him.*

-Genesis 2:18 (KJV)

*Then Samuel took a vial of oil, and poured it upon his head,
and kissed him, and said, Is it not because the Lord hath
anointed thee to be captain over his inheritance?*

*2 When thou art departed from me to day, then thou shalt
find two men by Rachel's sepulchre in the border of Benjamin
at Zelzah; and they will say unto thee, The asses which thou
wentest to seek are found: and, lo, thy father hath left the care
of the asses, and sorroweth for you, saying, What shall I do
for my son?*

*3 Then shalt thou go on forward from thence, and thou shalt
come to the plain of Tabor, and there shall meet thee three
men going up to God to Bethel, one carrying three kids, and
another carrying three loaves of bread, and another carrying
a bottle of wine:*

*4 And they will salute thee, and give thee two loaves of bread;
which thou shalt receive of their hands.*

5 After that thou shalt come to the hill of God, where is the

garrison of the Philistines: and it shall come to pass, when
thou art come thither to the city, that thou shalt meet a
company of prophets coming down from the high place with
a psaltery, and a tabret, and a pipe, and a harp, before them;
and they shall prophesy:

6 And the Spirit of the Lord will come upon thee, and thou
shalt prophesy with them, and shalt be turned into another
man.

1Samuel 10:1-6 (KJV)

Destiny is what God created you for in life and destiny is what you are sent to fulfil in life. But before this destiny can speak you need those who will show you the way and also those that will activate your destiny, they can be your prophet, your pastor, your boss, Man or woman, Old or young etc.

Prayer: I decree, enter into the hands of your destiny helper in Jesus name.

Three important people you will meet in life on the way to your destiny: *DESTINY KILLERS*, DESTINY SNATCHER, and *DESTINY HELPER*

Destiny Killers

Destiny killer will never want you to reach the top in live, they will never want to succeed or make it to the top in life.

Destiny Snatcher

They are the ones ready to steal your destiny.

You can't walk without coming across one of these two people, there is no one with a great destiny in life that will not meet one of these two people or even meet both of them.

> *Prayer:* Anyone you come across in life that want to kill your destiny or steal your destiny from you, or that has been using your destiny unknown to you will die suddenly.

> *Prayer:* I prophesy as an oracle of the most high God sent to you, anyone that is born of a woman, that want to steal or snatch or even kill your destiny will die suddenly.

King Herod wanted to kill the destiny of our Lord Jesus Christ and he used all his strength and power to terminate Jesus destiny. He drove Jesus out of town, to wilderness where destiny cannot speak.

> *Note:* once a destiny killer is not successful in killing or snatching your destiny from you they can shift you from where your helper is, they can deceive you and move you away from where your helper is.

There is no family that doesn't have these two set of people, destiny killer will never want you to outshine them.

How Can They Steal, Snatch or Collect Your Destiny from You?

- They will offer you a gift to collect your destiny

- They can go to the extent of implicating you in front of your helper

- They will go to any length in tarnishing your image to your destiny helper.

Note: If your pastor or prophet is your destiny helper they will turn your back at them and you begins to fight them and you end up under destiny killer, but I pray the mercy of God will bring your destiny out.

Destiny Helpers

This is the third category of people you must meet in life.

Prayer: The person that will make your destiny to be fulfilled I pray you enter into their hand from today in Jesus name.

Note: You don't need to labour for those who will assist you to be fulfilled in your destiny.

Prayer: Destiny helper that will cause a positive change in your life, wherever you are on the surface of the earth may God connect you with them in Jesus name.

Who are the Helpers of Destiny?

1. They are those who are ready to transform your life for good that will be vivid for eyes to see. Those that will transform your company, your academic, your marriage. I pray those who will cause your life to be transformed suddenly to a better destiny, you enter into their hands. Helper of destiny will not ask you what you need, they will do it without asking.

Prayer: Helper of destiny that will transform your life to better without asking you enter into their hands today in the mighty name of Jesus Christ.

2. Those that will cause your life to experience uncommon outstanding breakthrough.

Prayer: Those that will cause uncommon outstanding breakthrough in your life in your father's house, in your mother's house, wherever you are located all over the world, among men, among women enter into their hands today.

3. Those that will enlarge your coast for you.

Prayer: The mighty hand of the living God that will enlarge your coast appear in your life in the mighty name of Jesus Christ.

Prayer: I prophesy in the name of the father, son and Holy Ghost, enter into the hands of your destiny helper that will enlarge your coast, meet them from today, in Jesus name.

Let Us Pray

- In this month, come into my life. I want to experience your existence in my life in Jesus name.

- That person that will turn my life around for good this month Lord send them to me.

- That one man and woman that will show you the way to greatness, the connected way to riches in the mighty name of the father, son and Holy Spirit enter into their hands. *Genesis 37:14-17*

Note: When your life receive great turn around people that matter will follow you not crowd. Every evil covenants joining you with the crowd catch fire in Jesus name.

- Father send that person that will cause great turn around in my life in this new month man or woman, old or young send them to me, raise them for me.

- Father that person that will cause great turn around in my life in this new month be it man or woman, old or young wherever they are, God please go and help them for me in this month.

- Father destiny helper that will turn my destiny around for good let me meet them, raise them for me.

- Father those that will make me experience uncommon outstanding breakthrough, destiny helper, that will make me experience uncommon breakthrough father, son and Holy Ghost let me enter into their hands.

- Lord rise up and raise the person that will make me experience uncommon outstanding breakthrough. Father let me meet them, let me get in contact with them all over the world (mentioned your business name in the country you are).

Note: If you have not met with a destiny helper your beauty will fade away. In fact your handsomeness and beauty is nothing to write about until you meet with your destiny helper then your beauty and handsomeness will come out.

If your life lacks destiny helpers, life battles will convert you to what is not the plan of God for your life, but if you enter the hand of destiny helper that will make you experience uncommon outstanding breakthrough, you are victorious.

- Destiny helper that will enlarge my coast, that will be my burden bearer, that will enlarge my business, my marriage, my ministry whether white or black, raise them for me and send them to my life in this new month.

- Lord rise up in your power and strength, helper of destiny that will enlarge my coast and my life father help me locate them for my life wherever they are.

- Every arrow of the enemy denying you of destiny helpers catch fire.

- Every hand of the enemy stopping destiny helpers in your life catch fire.

- In this new month I meet my destiny helper in Jesus mighty name.

- Every power holding me down loose its grip and catches fire.

- First testimony in this month starts from my house and my life.

- The head of my problem loose their life for your life.

- Everything you have lost in the journey of life from beginning of the year, I decree recover all back in this month. Mercy will collect them back for you.

- In this month, you will be made head wherever you are, mercy of God will locate you.

- Receive good news that will end all your sorrow that will cause you to dance, mail and letter of good news is coming your way in this month.

- Man like angel and angel like man that your life and destiny needs, you will meet with in Jesus name.

- Those destiny helpers who will meet all your needs white or black, old or young, that will meet your need financially, in good health, in getting a good job, meet them today.

- Helper of destiny that you don't know where they came from begin to meet them in Jesus mighty name.

- Helper that will not consider your error without helping you meet them in Jesus mighty name.

- Every junction of your life that is a battle point, this month you will not be stopped. And anyone having a charge case will be favoured and it will end in joy for you.

- Everything you have been expecting for past months, with mercy they are released to you today, I say receive a good news, in Jesus name.

- Miracles that will change your story that will change the level you are operating at receive these miracles today, you will be favoured.

Note: The ancient of days direct my path this month.

CHAPTER 2

Destiny Helper

I decree, a destiny helper that will use all that he has to help you without looking at your past, incapability, failures, weakness and all of that, you shall be connected to such helper in the name of Jesus.

What is Destiny? We would look at it from two sides.

1. The purpose you are created for by God.

2. What God assigned you to do on earth.

Something can be created because of a particular person, at the long run the person may not be able to use it.

Secondly what one is assigned to do. This book is created for a purpose which is why you are reading it. I remember a renowned gospel Artist, *Dr Bisi Alawiye – Aluko* in one of her albums, where she sang *"Oni Idi kan Olorun mi to fi dami si aye"* meaning *"there is a particular purpose, God created me for on earth"*.

The mystery here is that before your destiny can speak or function, one can't do it alone. You needs a PATHFINDER and also an ACTIVATOR or a STARTER. Imagine this scenario where you buy a brand-new iPhone or an Android phone, you need to power it up, download series of apps on the phone and by that you will be able to go deep and deeper to fully utilise the phone. Similarly, in one's life, a destiny activator or starter is needed which could either be a Prophet, Pastor, Mallams (Alfa), a benefactor, a man a woman, etc. They would be the one to show you the way or activate your destiny.

> *I prophesy, The Destiny helper that will show you the way to reach your destination and way out of the storms, calamities and afflictions, shall be connected to you in the name of Jesus Amen.*

In the journey of destiny, two personalities are always a must on your path.

1. Destiny Killers or Destiny Robbers.

2. Destiny Helpers or Destiny Fulfillers.

Destiny Killers or Destiny Robbers

No destiny carrier that doesn't come across destiny killers or robbers.

> *Prayer: Listen, everyone killing or robbing you of your destiny shall be declared dead, in Jesus name.*

No household without destiny killers or robbers. King Herod is the destiny killer that was after Jesus Christ. He used all that were within his reach to see that he kills the destiny of Jesus Christ our Lord. He sent Jesus out of town into the wilderness, into the land of slavery where destinies don't talk. Just like the life of many, the battle of their destiny killers has chased many people to where they are not supposed to be. In one of my messages that the Lord inspired me to preach, *"Entering The Wrong Vehicle."* Destiny killers or robbers are not always far from destiny carriers but when they see that they are unable to kill the owner of the destiny, they send them away from where the destiny is designed to speak or function. They have different means to attack or stop destinies from speaking, setup battles, court cases, sickness, etc.

In the book of *Matthew 2:1-20 (KJV)*,

1 Now when Jesus was born in Bethlehem of Judea in the days of Herod the king, behold, there came wise men from the East to Jerusalem,

2 saying, "Where is He that is born King of the Jews? For we have seen His star in the East and have come to worship Him."

3 When Herod the king had heard these things, he was troubled, and all Jerusalem with him.

4 And when he had gathered all the chief priests and scribes of the people together, he demanded of them where Christ should be born.

5 And they said unto him, "In Bethlehem of Judea, for thus it is written by the prophet:

6 *'And thou, Bethlehem, in the land of Judah, art not the least among the princes of Judah; for out of thee shall come a Governor, that shall rule My people Israel.'"*

7 *Then Herod, when he had privily called the wise men, inquired of them diligently what time the star appeared.*

8 *And he sent them to Bethlehem and said, "Go and search diligently for the young child, and when ye have found him, bring me word again, that I may come and worship him also."*

9 *When they had heard the king, they departed; and lo, the star which they saw in the East went before them until it came and stood over where the young Child was.*

10 *When they saw the star, they rejoiced with exceeding great joy.*

11 *And when they had come into the house, they saw the young Child with Mary His mother, and fell down and worshipped Him. And when they had opened their treasures, they presented unto Him gifts: gold and frankincense and myrrh.*

12 *And being warned by God in a dream that they should not return to Herod, they departed into their own country another way.*

13 *And when they had departed, behold, the angel of the Lord appeared to Joseph in a dream, saying, "Arise, and take the young Child and His mother, and flee into Egypt, and be thou there until I bring thee word; for Herod will seek the young Child to destroy Him."*

14 When he arose, he took the young Child and His mother by night and departed into Egypt,

15 and was there until the death of Herod, that it might be fulfilled which was spoken of the Lord by the prophet, saying, "Out of Egypt have I called My Son."

16 Then Herod, when he saw that he was mocked by the wise men, was exceeding wroth, and sent forth and slew all the children who were in Bethlehem and in all the region thereof, from two years old and under, according to the time which he had diligently inquired of the wise men.

17 Then was fulfilled that which was spoken by Jeremiah the prophet, saying,

18 "In Ramah was there a voice heard, lamentation and weeping and great mourning, Rachel weeping for her children and would not be comforted, because they are no more."

19 But when Herod was dead, behold, an angel of the Lord appeared in a dream to Joseph in Egypt,

20 saying, "Arise, and take the young Child and His mother, and go into the land of Israel, for they are dead who sought the young Child's life." Herod, chased Jesus out of his place of birth all in a bid to stop His destiny from speaking.

Moses destiny was attacked by Pharaoh. Pharaoh instructs that every male child be killed in the land of Egypt.

Characteristics of destiny killers, just as the case of Pharaoh here is that they don't want people to multiply or increase in number. They dislike seeing people surpass them in anything and hate to see people grow. They dislike people going far achieving and surpassing many more goals than themselves, so if you have a great destiny, you must be prepared in all areas because opposition will be raised to kill that destiny.

See Book of *Exodus 1:7-22 (KJV)*,

> *7 And the children of Israel were fruitful and increased abundantly, and multiplied, and waxed exceeding mighty; and the land was filled with them.*

> *8 Now there arose up a new king over Egypt, who knew not Joseph.*

> *9 And he said unto his people, "Behold, the people of the children of Israel are more and mightier than we.*

> *10 Come on, let us deal wisely with them, lest they multiply and it come to pass, when there befalleth any war, that they join also unto our enemies and fight against us, and so get them up out of the land."*

> *11 Therefore they set over them taskmasters to afflict them with their burdens. And they built for Pharaoh treasure cities, Pithom and Raamses.*

> *12 But the more they afflicted them, the more they multiplied and grew; and they were grieved because of the children of Israel.*

> *13 And the Egyptians made the children of Israel to serve with rigour.*

14 And they made their lives bitter with hard bondage, in mortar and in brick and in all manner of service in the field; all their service wherein they made them serve was with rigor.

15 And the king of Egypt spoke to the Hebrew midwives, of whom the name of one was Shiphrah, and the name of the other Puah.

16 And he said, "When ye do the office of a midwife to the Hebrew women and see them upon the birthstools, if it be a son then ye shall kill him; but if it be a daughter then she shall live."

17 But the midwives feared God, and did not do as the king of Egypt commanded them, but saved the men children alive.

18 And the king of Egypt called for the midwives and said unto them, "Why have ye done this thing, and have saved the men children alive?"

19 And the midwives said unto Pharaoh, "Because the Hebrew women are not as the Egyptian women; for they are lively, and are delivered ere the midwives come in unto them."

20 Therefore God dealt well with the midwives, and the people multiplied and waxed very mighty.

21 And it came to pass, because the midwives feared God, that He made them houses.

22 And Pharaoh charged all his people, saying, "Every son who is born ye shall cast into the river, and every daughter ye shall save alive."

Destiny Killers or Robbers; Modus Operandi

- Gifts presenting you with a gift in order to take destiny away from you.

- Implicating and setting up Destiny Carriers: They through discussion or interaction reporting destroy, deform characters or character assassination of destiny carriers

- Condemnation: Destiny robbers, implicate, can also condemn or share wrong information about one in the presence of your helper. Take for instance, a lady that is in courtship can be tarnished by destiny robbers. Or if it is the pastor/prophet that is your destiny helper, the destiny robber can create enmity between the pastor / prophet and the destiny carrier would end up with the people that will not enable the fulfilment of destiny. Many are in this kind of position. I Pray as many of you that are in this kind of situation, mercy will deliver your lives out of such situation in the name of Jesus.

Destiny Helpers or Destiny Fulfillers

Let me start by praying, Be you a man or a woman reading this book, the good vision that you have, good thought in your mind that you desire or plan to execute, that which will make it happen, the person that you will meet that will make the vision come to fulfilment in the name of the Father, Son and the Holy Spirit, be connected to such a person in Jesus name.

Some years back, I used to hold a radio programme in Lagos every Tuesday. After the programme one fateful day, I prayed this prayer *"the champion of your battle be pushed into the fire, garment of battle on you be consumed by fire."* A listener heard this, visited the radio station that she wants to meet with the man that prayed the above prayer over the radio that the prayer was directed to her problems so she want to bless that man of God and that she wants to do something that will last him at least some years. The program anchor suggested to her, that how about using the prayer for caller ring back tunes, the woman bought the idea and I was contacted, if I can pray such kind of prayer under a minute. I replied *"I can pray it for an hour if that is what you want."* I in turn asked what is all this about? And the response I got was not to worry he would revert. I was curious, so I did about 3 types and sent to him and the lady took them to telecoms service providers(MTN, ETISALAT, GLO and AIRTEL) they signed agreement to use it as caller ring back tune and one Sunday morning some documents were brought to me that I should sign which I did I remember seeing 30% against my name, the company and the lady also get their percentage. I was saying to myself the money will assist me in continuous propagation of the gospel over the radio. After the third month from the time I signed I began to receive credit notification every month. One day I was in Lagos and I saw on TVC where the tune was rated among the first ten in the rating of top caller tunes. For good four years I was getting very good support in the ministry through that caller tune. Don't forget I never prayed for this woman directly neither have I met with her, but she was a destiny helper.

CHAPTER 3

Why You Must Fulfil Destiny

What is Destiny? Destiny is what God created you for and what he sent you to do in life after creating you. If God created you for a purpose and you couldn't fulfil the purpose for which he created you, you have disappointed him and He won't be happy with you. You won't only have disappointed God but also the set of people he sent you.

People you will disappoint if you don't fulfil destiny:

1. Your Creator (GOD)

2. Your parents

3. Your Husband/wife and Children

4. Your city where you came from

5.   And the person that you are sent to in life, people that God want them to become somebody in life through you.

> *Note: If your parents didn't pray some people will never allow you to have rest of mind, we always pray that God should send us our destiny helper and also send us to our destiny helper.*

Some people do pray that *'anyone that is meant to help me, FATHER don't let he or she have rest of mind'* but you have failed to understand that you suppose to help someone too but you're yet to. If your destiny is not working nor yet fulfilled, people can kill you with their prayer if you have not yet fulfilled your purpose for their lives.

> *Note: A lot of people that are lunatic didn't fulfil their purpose in life while some even fulfil it than many who are normal in nature.*

In *1 Samuel 10:1-6 (KJV)*,

> *1 Then Samuel took a vial of oil and poured it upon his head, and kissed him and said, "Is it not because the Lord hath anointed thee to be captain over His inheritance?*
>
> *2 When thou art departed from me today, then thou shalt find two men by Rachel's sepulcher in the border of Benjamin at Zelzah; and they will say unto thee, 'The asses which thou wentest to seek are found. And lo, thy father hath left the care of the asses and sorroweth for you, saying, "What shall I do for my son?"'*

3 Then shalt thou go on forward from thence, and thou shalt come to the plain of Tabor; and there shall meet thee three men going up to God at Bethel, one carrying three kids and another carrying three loaves of bread and another carrying a bottle of wine.

4 And they will salute thee and give thee two loaves of bread, which thou shalt receive from their hands.

5 After that thou shalt come to the hill of God, where is the garrison of the Philistines; and it shall come to pass, when thou art come thither to the city, that thou shalt meet a company of prophets coming down from the high place with a psaltery and a taboret and a pipe and a harp before them; and they shall prophesy.

6 And the Spirit of the Lord will come upon thee, and thou shalt prophesy with them and shalt be turned into another man.

Here something was lost in the hands of Saul and he is looking for it and he met the prophet why? Because he obeyed; it was his servant who advised him. He told the servant he has nothing to offer the prophet but the servant said he has little things to give the prophet. Never go to a prophet's house with empty hand. The servant pushed his master, you also need someone that will push you and God has raised me up to push you for you to know you have a destiny.

Saul wouldn't have suffered like that if he had put God first. So, also, many believe in their own righteousness and never put GOD first would have already taken a step before seeking the face of GOD ; and this makes us miss it in the journey of our destiny.

Likewise servants of GOD must not take a step without seeking the face of GOD first. That HE (GOD) called us doesn't mean we should not seek GOD'S face first. GOD sent Jethro to Moses, likewise, I am sent to some destinies in time like this.

Saul was not from king's lineage but Samuel who anointed him was operating like the king or the judge by that time. However, the people kept demanding for a king (in emulation to other nations).With this, Samuel had to anoint Saul; made known to him his as a king. But Saul been full of himself passed his boundary and took on himself the duty of a prophet. And he chose never to listen to the one who had chosen him as a king.

Saul would have lasted as king because the anointing of Samuel on him worked as a prophet, as a king and as a judge –that is, the auction of the anointing was transferred from Samuel to him. 'Glory rose through another glory'.

Prayer: *Anointing that will move your destiny forward will be poured on you today.*

Everything the prophet said was fulfilled and all the instructions given. Verse 3, because of the little gift he brought to the prophet he received double. Many don't want to sow to their destiny.

You have to bring your sacrifice and service to the people at the top for you to reach the top. Never think you won't sow for the people at the top if you desire to reach the top. Many destinies have been lost and the only thing that can fetch it out or locate it is obedience and seed. The Bible says in *Psalm 126:5* that those who sow in tears will reap with joy. When you sow you won't know when you will sow to your destiny helper. We see Abraham as a good example. He saw the angel of God and took care of them and they spoke to their destiny that this time next year they will have their own child.

The step you will take for your destiny to be good in life is in your hand, Saul obeyed his servant and things changed for him, his life was turned around.

The Duties of Destiny Helper in a Man's Life

1. **Destiny helper will connect you with people at the top.** It's not good to take someone as a spiritual father or mother and your life has no value to them. A true life story of our Father in the Lord, Prophet Sam Olu-Alo. Helper of destiny don't give you money alone to help you but they use their position to connect you with people at the top. Your destiny helper must be able to interpret your dream.

2. **Destiny helper will turn you to a valuable person(will add value to your life)/ turn your destiny to be priceless.** Its some people that will lift you up and add value to your life, then you become priceless. Your life and destiny will be changed and value will be added to your life.

> **Prayer:** *Helper of destiny that will add value to your life and destiny you will meet them and they will meet you in life both home and abroad.*

Despite your qualification because your life lacks a destiny helper, not much value is added to your life but once there is a destiny helper in your life, your destiny value will increase.

No matter your calling you still need a destiny helper that will add value to your life. Many destinies don't appreciate anything that people do for them so their destinies lack destiny helpers.

3.   **They will help /assist you to have breakthrough.** They sometimes scold you and correct all your errors. They will use everything in their possession, power and capacity to help your destiny to succeed. Also they will use all their wisdom to guide you and protect you because they know once you die many other glory carriers connected to you may die or suffer set backs. Many destinies would have succeeded in life but their life lack destiny helpers. They are surrounded by people that will cause their down fall, so it's difficult for them to succeed in life.

4.   **Those that will be your burden bearer.** Your burden they would take upon themselves as if you are their sibling. They are even ready to die for you if it causes them their life. They will treat you even better than their own people and take up your matter personally.

5.   **Those that will use all their power, strength and everything they have to remove every hindrance on your way.** Theses are people that will not allow anything to truncate your destiny or anything that might not allow your destiny to be fulfilled. They are there to remove every obstacle, removing anything that can stop you from reaching the top. They will never allow anything to hinder you reaching the top.

As a destiny carrier, when you are unable to fulfil your destiny, you will have failed 6 different stakeholders of your life: God, your parents, spouse, children, your town and the person(s) whom you are sent to. Always say this prayer as a destiny carrier:

Lord don't let me fail you, my parent, spouse, children, my town and the person am sent to in name of Jesus.

Now, you need to understand the implication of this. If your parents are not the praying type, remember that you are praying God push me into the hand of my destiny helper. There are also some people that the prayer they offer on their knees at the mountain top is that *"O Lord, wherever my destiny helper is please seize or take sleep away from him, make him restless until he locates me."* Who is this prayer targeted at? None other than You. Do you know that at times the challenges that you are passing through might be as a result of some people's prayers. Remember in the Bible *Esther 6 : 1 (KJV)*

> *On that night could not the king sleep, and he commanded to bring the book of records of the chronicles; and they were read before the king.*

You will see that the king couldn't sleep because of Mordecai. His sleeplessness led him to request the chronicles be brought forward and there he found Mordecai was yet to be honoured for a good deed done the king. So we have people that you are sent to that can use their prayers to push and pull you. As such, it is very important your destiny is fulfilled as well as meet the people you are destined to raise.

Let us quickly read, the *1 Samuel 10:1-6 (KJV)*,

> *1 Then Samuel took a vial of oil and poured it upon his head, and kissed him and said, "Is it not because the Lord hath anointed thee to be captain over His inheritance?*
>
> *2 When thou art departed from me today, then thou shalt find two men by Rachel's sepulcher in the border of Benjamin at Zelzah; and they will say unto thee, 'The asses which thou wentest to seek are found. And lo, thy father hath left the care of the asses and sorroweth for you, saying, "What shall I do for my son?"'*
>
> *3 Then shalt thou go on forward from thence, and thou shalt come to the plain of Tabor; and there shall meet thee three men going up to God at Bethel, one carrying three kids and another carrying three loaves of bread and another carrying a bottle of wine.*
>
> *4 And they will salute thee and give thee two loaves of bread, which thou shalt receive from their hands.*
>
> *5 After that thou shalt come to the hill of God, where is the garrison of the Philistines; and it shall come to pass, when thou art come thither to the city, that thou shalt meet a company of prophets coming down from the high place with a psaltery and a taboret and a pipe and a harp before them; and they shall prophesy.*
>
> *6 And the Spirit of the Lord will come upon thee, and thou shalt prophesy with them and shalt be turned into another man.*

I most not fail to tell you this. One of my fathers in the Lord said to me that he had a revelation concerning me, where I was giving offering to the less privileged people and I was tired and sweating. At that point, a small boy appeared and was consoling me telling me you are trying and tired. It would have been better you look for someone who has, sow in his life and continuously do it and never one day think that this person has and you won't give to him or her again for the very moment you begin to do that then you won't get to your destination. In this revelation, my spirit bore witness to it, though my flesh also doubted it seriously. Finally, I succumb to the Spirit of God and transferred the whole amount in my account ₦102,000.00, to this man of God. Upon receipt, he said to me I did not tell you so you can give me money , but since you have done this you will not stress again and God will surprise you. Not long after, my town where I left with one shirt and trouser with bathroom slippers, I built a small apartment under two months when I gave out that money on me as a sacrificial deed. I am only explaining further what it is, when you sow you will reap. See in *1 Samuel 9*, Saul and his servant took just little cake to the prophet and he got more than he bargained for. See what happened in *1 Samuel 10:1-4*.

One of the things a destiny helper does is to connect you. One fateful day, one of my fathers, Baba Gideon Obiwale was supposed to attend a meeting at Ikeji Arakeji, but he was indisposed to attend the programme so he asked me to represent him. I was very skinny and tiny then. I went with Pastor Segun Oyebola. When it was Baba Obiwale's turn to minister, the coordinator said to me being his representative that I have just forty minutes because they still have more programme to cover. Before I was handed the microphone I called on Pastor Segun and we prayed fervently for seven minutes, I was sweating profusely before the man called on us to the altar. For the first five minutes I didn't know what to say, suddenly an angel of God touched me, I called the name of Jesus and the whole place was on fire. I ministered for two hours wherein I was given forty minutes. I called on the elders that were seated on the altar they were nowhere to be found. All I heard them say was that the Lord would have you continue. After we finished the ministration, they were amazed and the ovation was loud, the Lord honoured both Pastor Segun and I, even among our friends. Since that day, our lives have never being the same. Don't forget destiny helpers connects.

Another instance was in the presence of Baba Joe Jacob. A youth programme was up in Ikeji Arakeji. I am a full member of CAC, a product of CAC school of Prophets and Seminary, so I know the doctrine that it is never permissible when your lead or superior has finished ministering for you as a junior to repeat prayer points already prayed by the elder. So this fateful day, Baba Gideon Obiwale was the one that asked me to come along with him to the youth programme. He delivered a powerful ministration and it was time for us to leave the venue of the programme. Suddenly he stood up danced for the Lord and collected the microphone to announce "I am now going to invite one of CAC, dynamic Prophet in the person of Prophet Sam Olu-Alo." I wasn't expecting that but to the glory of God I don't get intimidated when it comes to doing the work of God. Suddenly, my eyes changed, I was deep in prayers. When I received the microphone I raised a song, *"Arise, Arise, Arise, the calling of my fathers that have slept in the Lord, arise ,arise, arise."* Brethren before I finished that song, the Holy spirit came down and the entire place was on fire. O what a marvellous father, Baba Obiwale was very happy and proud, and was nodding in appreciation to God and Baba Joe Jacob was filled with surprise.

Ever since that day my life has never remained the same. It is not only money that destiny helpers will offer you. At times, they will connect you with the people at the top. I told one of my acquaintances that your father in the Lord might not be able to dream for you but he must be able to interpret your dreams and that has nothing to do with age.

Sometimes in 2014, I was in America with CAC General Evangelist on a crusade. After he finished ministering at the programme, he stood up and said a young man is here and he is the one chosen by God to pray over all the prayers that we have offered this moment. I replied to him Baba you have prayed, he said to me that is the voice of God not him, so I obeyed.

I have a lot to tell you… you need a destiny helper.

When I was still learning the bricklaying trade, there was a man who usually comes from Abuja, and he beseeched my boss to quote for a housing project in Abuja. My boss initially quoted the traditional Ado Ekiti pricing but his friend advised him to quote professionally bearing in mind Abuja is a higher priced city being the Federal Capital Territory. In the long run, my boss was awarded the contract of one of the housing units because he quoted a cost that was 50% of the Abuja contractors. He was still rejoicing that he has won a big contract. Upon completion the Abuja contractors were shocked to see the quality of the structure built by us. After that job, my boss was rated higher and his value increased. He thereafter moved from State to State in Nigeria to build additional housing projects.

Destiny helpers will use all they have to assist you and see that you have a breakthrough and wherever you have deficiencies or need improvement they will tell you. Also, if you don't desist from certain things, they will tell you where you are not supposed to do certain things, they will advise you against it. If you don't have the right attire and they want to take you to a certain place of honour, they will dress you.

In Ikeja, Lagos a woman was planning her daughter's wedding and desired for me to minister at the wedding alongside another guest minister from South Africa. My initial reaction was to allow me attend as a guest and not minister especially since I am not fluent in English. But she replied and said "even the battles and challenges of my life too cannot speak English." So when the programme started, the woman, requested the microphone from the Master of Ceremony and she said to the invited guests in English that "I want Prophet of God to pray for me in Yoruba, because my battle cannot speak English, also the battle/affliction my daughter's father, who is my husband don't understand English, so I want him to bless us with the spirit of God upon his life." The MC was shocked at what she said. I was then handed the microphone and I called the name of Jesus, God of the prophets and even the guests on high heels were bowing to the ground in worship of God. After the prayers, people started saying "no wonder this is where you are hiding. We also will locate him, we will take his contact, we must go look for him." Do you already have such people in your life?

We also have destiny helpers that will surround you and their goal is to make you successful. Many gubernatorial and presidential aspirants have the wrong people, the people that will push them down or cause them to trip surrounding them.

Another duty of destiny helpers is that they stand by you and personally take up what belongs to you as though you are one of their siblings. They can lay their lives down for you. I remember a particular road trip with my driver Sunny when armed robbers were attacking on the road I called his attention and he said, Daddy you just bend down your head and lo and behold he sped past that point and I said to him how did you do that? His response was, *"daddy nothing must touch you."* He was not afraid of his life but he was bent on saving me. Others were robbed that day.

Destiny helpers will use all their strength to remove every obstruction on your way and they will ensure they remove every obstruction from your way. For they know that if you do certain things it will have a multiplier effect. See for example, when Sani Abacha died, some people's destinies were affected. When Abiola also died, some people's destinies too were truncated.

Summary of duties of destiny helpers to destiny Carriers.

1.   They connect you to the people at the top

2.   They give you higher value or highly priced.

3.   They will assist you to have breakthrough

4.   Destiny helper will stand by you like a sibling, and lay-down their lives for you.

5.   Destiny helpers will use their strength to remove every obstruction or hindrance from your way.

Now the question is that the above listed destiny helpers, are they present in your life, your spouse or children's life?

Let Us Pray

- If you are so inclined you can include fasting with this prayer or appoint some days to and fast and pray.

- Call the name of Jesus three times, Lord come in to my life you and the destiny helper you created to help me.

- Call the name of Jesus three time, every sin that stops destiny helpers from locating me, Lord forgive me of my sins.

- Call the name of Jesus threes time, Helpers that will connect me with the people at the top (mention your name) I am connected with that person.

- Call the name of Jesus three times, hear the word of God my (Mention your Name) destiny, go and be connected with the people that will connect me with the people at the top.

- Call the name of Jesus three times, you my destiny go and be connected with those that will make you have higher value in the society.

- Call the name of Jesus, those that will support me to be successful at what God has destined me to do, let my destiny be connected with them.

- Father come into my life with the destiny helper you have for my destiny.

- Father every sin denying me of destiny helper wash my sins away.

- Father destiny helper that will connect my destiny with people at the top I (mention your name) be connected to him/her.

- Lord I (mention your name) am connected to the people that will connect my destiny with people at the top.

- My destiny, my calling, my ministry be connected with my destiny helper at the top.

- My destiny, hear the word of the Lord, go and locate my destiny helper that will add value to my life.

Note: *Without a destiny helper, your destiny may never be fulfilled.*

- My destiny, my life meet the destiny helpers that will help me to be lifted and connect me to people at the top.

End by reading Psalm 20:1-end.

CHAPTER 4

Destiny Helpers
You Need in Your Life

1. Those that will bring changes (noticeable changes) to your life.

2. Those that will make you have an uncommon breakthrough.

3. Those that will expand your coast

Elisha, as a prophet during his time believed they can make do with whatever thing or space available to them, but among the sons of prophet said to him see *2 Kings 1-2(KJV)*

> *1 And the sons of the prophets said unto Elisha, Behold now, the place where we dwell with thee is too strait for us. 2 Let us go, we pray thee, unto Jordan, and take thence every man a beam, and let us make us a place there, where we may dwell. And he answered, Go ye.*

I pray a destiny helper that will use his money/idea/advise to expand your business, your work, ministry, career,life, shall be connected with you in Jesus name. Amen.

The likes that will come up to you and tell you take this 2 million or 20 million add to your business, and goes like when are you able to return it? If your response is I don't know yet he won't be bothered and in fact he might end up saying to you don't bother to pay back.

I have a prophet friend, a man came to him sometime ago that the Lord has instructed him to be paying the tithe of his company to the prophet friend of mine and this man here has not yet built a church not even a plot of land but the first tithe that was giving to this man was N250 million. Suddenly the man bought the entire place where they were worshipping. The man promised to continue paying the company tithe to the prophet's ministry. The prophet went further to get in touch with old, aged and grey headed men of God, he bought them cars, placed them on salaries so that their prayers would sustain this Oil of blessing. What happened to this prophet? He was connected with his destiny helper that expanded his coast.

I speak in the name of the Father, Son and the Holy Spirit destiny helpers that will expand your coast, that will take you from your current level to the next level, you shall be connected with them in Jesus name.

I prayed for a man and the Lord told me to tell him when he gets married his coast will be expanded, so also another man, I told him that he needs a woman in his life , the moment he got married, his life skyrocketed,

Listen, that person that your life needs that will cause your coast to be expanded, who will take you from the position of

emptiness to a glorious position, you shall be connected with that person, in the name of Jesus. Amen.

Genesis 37:14-17

14 And he said to him, "Go, I pray thee, see whether it be well with thy brethren and well with the flocks, and bring me word again." So he sent him out of the Vale of Hebron, and he came to Shechem.

15 And a certain man found him, and behold, he was wandering in the field; and the man asked him, saying, "What seekest thou?"

16 And he said, "I seek my brethren. Tell me, I pray thee, where they feed their flocks."

17 And the man said, "They have departed hence, for I heard them say, 'Let us go to Dothan.'" And Joseph went after his brethren, and found them in Dothan.

From verse 15 of the Genesis 37, where it says

"And a certain man found him." a destiny helper that will find you to help you shall locate you in Jesus name.

"And he was wandering in the field." A destiny helper who will find you were you are wandering without you showing yourself will locate you for help in Jesus name. Your life needs someone that will find/identify you. Some years back after I finished from a crusade in Europe I had a connecting flight so a pastor friend was asking me to pay attention because the intervals

are too short when the flights are announced and if care is not taken I might miss the flight. I listened but not taken that into consideration much, I was on a call when I walked past the gate that I was supposed to board from. Also, unknown to me, the flight time had being changed so I was feeling bad and dejected thinking that I have missed my flight. Suddenly a man came up to me and said *"You resemble a prophet that has once prayed for me, you went as far as emptying your pocket and gave me all the money you had on you then and spoke the word that the world (Mankind) will use me as a prayer point because of the kind of mighty change that will happen in my life."* I couldn't utter anything other than *"can you speak Yoruba"* that was the question I asked him because I see myself to have missed my flight, he responded affirmatively and added *"you said during the time you were praying that in three year's time the change will be so visible."* I couldn't remember but it is in my character to do such at times to people, since I am only God's mouthpiece. I quickly said to him I have missed my flight I am returning to that place where you said I have prayed for you. He then inquired which flight, so I handed him the Air France ticket I had on me and he said he too is on same flight that the flight was delayed, that I am still on time.

Having realised that I have not missed the flight he began asking questions, he requested to see my seat position on the air plane and I was on economy while he was on business. He said to me *"you must be tired from the crusade you just finished, so you need a better place, I will give you my seat while I take yours."* I thanked him, when we boarded he showed me how to adjust the seat so I will be able to lay on my back and take some sleep to reboot my system, he then left for his seat which was meant to be mine. I knelt down, prayed and I felt a hand touch me and said to me you did not know that man, I am the one that sent an angel to you. But if you want to be sure go the original seat meant for you see who is on it. Brethren, when I got to the place where I was supposed to sit no single black person was among the people sitting in that area of the plane. Then the Lord said to me, *"son it is because of what you do, that is why I have decided to visit you by sending you an angel."*

Brethren, you have to pay the price, sacrifice to get to higher places, to have your destiny fulfilled or to even get connected to destiny helpers but many of us are not ready to pay the price. Remember Joseph agreed to go check on his brothers where they had gone to feed the flocks on the request of his father. This was the price he paid, agreeing to go, that was where he entered into slavery. When there are no suffering/challenges there can't be glory as the case of many that never want to suffer but want to be glorious. When you have no history your light can't shine and if you shine it won't last long before your star dimes. If you desire to shine till old age, then you must be connected with certain types of people in your life, some of which I have mentioned above but you will still read more about the destiny helpers you must have in your life.

4. Pathfinders

Pastors, Prophet, Businessmen and women, artisans etc, you need a person that will show or direct you to the path you need to tow to get to your destination.

Gen. 37:6

And he said, I seek my brethren: tell me, I pray thee, where they feed their flocks.

Many have lost or missed their destiny helpers because of pride, boastfulness, arrogance, etc. Joseph at this point begged and pleaded for the man to show him where his brothers were and he showed him the way.

A lot of destiny carriers are surrounded by a large crowd, most of which they take as destiny helpers, but they are destiny robbers, killers, imposters, destiny enslavers, destiny delayers, destiny changers, destiny trappers, etc. Most often, as a destiny carrier, having all these people around you will stop or delay you. A destiny carrier is created with its own government but when stuck with these kind of people, your destiny is trapped, as such you need one that will show you the path to follow or choose. Let me give you a very good example of this kind of personality. Our President, Muhammadu Buhari attempted to get to the seat three times but all to no avail but when he got the pathfinder, he got to the seat. Remember he was surrounded by crowd but not the right people. When he met with Asiwaju Bola Ahmed Tinubu, he was able to get to the office. Similarly, a person can be destined for a position or a particular place or thing but can be a slave because the right people are not with him or he is not with the right people.

You reading this book, yes, you, I know you have a big vision or idea inside of you but you are wandering like Joseph in the wilderness, until a pathfinder found him, that pathfinder that will find you and show you the path to where you need to be.

Today be connected to that person in the name of Jesus.

During the COVID-19 global lockdown, in one of our online programmes with some of my children in the Lord, I jokingly asked one of them that in the time past you normally give me lots of money but whenever you are leaving, I would in turn, give you a little, did you notice anything? That was my question to him and he responded that things were very well then with him but since he has stopped it he wasn't getting such. I said to him that what I was giving to you in the physical is small but in the spirit it is much bigger and it opens doors for you. So in your life you need someone that will show you the way, a pathfinder. Joseph suffered until he meet with a pathfinder, he has something to offer but couldn't deliver it because he has not gotten to where he would deliver it, same thing applies to you, you have an idea, you are a master in certain things but you are unable to find the pathfinders you need.

5. Destiny Promoters

This type of destiny helpers connect you with the people at the top most positions, people that matter, those at the helm of affair, those that are already and even surpass where you desire to be. Take for example, if Bola Ahmed Tinubu sends a letter to the present governor of Lagos state stating that the bearer be considered for a particular slot. If there are 100 people vying for same position who do you think the governor would pick, I want you to answer that in your mind. Though it is just a joke or an assumption I never said it happened.

So if you have an idea inside of you and you are unable to meet or find a destiny helper that will connect you to those at the top, the idea will just waste or die inside you when no one is there to connect you with people that matter. Many are supposed to be on the seat of the governor of a particular state but when they lack destiny helpers the vision was wasted since there was no one to connect them to the people at the top and when such a person dies, automatically the destiny will not be fulfilled, it becomes wasted.

In Lagos state some years back, I visited a company belonging to one my sons in the Lord, I think the time I visited that company was in January, first week of January to be precise and lots of people were outside waiting for an interview. As I was through with my prayers in the company on my way out, among the candidates that came for the interview greeted me using our local dialect and I answered. He said this is my father, I pitied him and I said to the owner of the company this man is from Ekiti, please assist him by giving him a job. The owner said, *"you hardly ask me for favours, I will honour you and give him a job."* He then asked if I knew him before now and he (the candidate) quickly answered that I am his prophet and father. That is how he was given a position meant for someone with a Masters degree though he possessed an Ordinary National Diploma (OND) at the time. You can see the gap but that was not taken into consideration because he got someone that connected him with the people that matter. After sometime, I met with the man and I asked him where exactly he hails from, he told me where he came from and that town is very far from my town. So I replied, *"you said we were from the same place which means you stylishly lied"*, he said, *"no sir, your God did it for me."* We laughed over it.

Many are in America, Europe and different parts of the world, yet you are still suffering because there is non to connect you to the people in higher places. Abroad where you are we see nationals of these countries who write wills for pets, are you saying God cannot connect you with such kinds of people that will be ready to help you with anything. There also exist your country nationals in that place that are not willing to help you, because these people are not sent to you, yet you glue yourself to them. You need to pray to get connected to your destiny helpers.

In the Bible *2 Kings 5*, there is a man of valour named Naaman, who through him God gave victory to Syria though he is a leper. A little maid that was brought in captivity from the land of Israel who was with Naaman's wife approached the master's wife and suggested that Naaman for visit the prophet that he will be cured of his sickness. The wife knelt down before her husband and asked him to go see the prophet and he heeded her advice. If you are a destiny carrier and you don't listen to advise your destiny will not come to pass. Observe the people in higher positions, you will hear they have personal advisers on different matters. Naaman went to the King but the King cannot offer him anything so he connects him with the Prophet by giving him a letter to the prophet of God (Elisha).

I have a sister in America, who shared one of our online programmes with a colleague and the person inquired if she knows me, and she said to her, *"he is my father in the Lord."*

Then the colleague said she has being trying to reach me for 7 years or more but couldn't reach me so she said to her how to reach me and asked her to go with her picture for proof and easier identification. When she came to where I was the crowd was so much, she just waved the picture in the air and said your daughter extends her greeting waving the picture in the air so it caught my attention. So I beckoned on her to come. I prayed for her, and I told her the Lord told me you are looking for fruit of the womb and she began to cry. I said to her *"you told me you wanted to greet me."* She said to me she has being looking to meet me for a long time. Now she has a child to the glory of God. This didn't happen until someone connected her to the person that her life needs.

6. Destiny Pillars or Support

These are the destiny support that your ladder of destiny will rest on to enable you climb. A ladder cannot stand on its own, it requires a support to rest on to enable it be suitable for you to climb. So it must lean on something before you can climb. Recently, I went to the place of prayer, I met with one elder in the Lord, and during the discussion with him, he referred to a brother that if he offends anyone he would go ahead and plead on his behalf because this brother will stand for him as well. In another discussion, a reference was made about certain set of people, that those people in question had support of XYZ and that is why they never seems to have any problem regarding financing as these people are ready to spend any amount to support this people in question. It was also concluded that they have people that give them financial support.

This is saying that a destiny cannot speak if it never has a support where the destiny owner can lean on. You should imagine when a ladder stands, it's usually checked to be sure if it is standing properly and can carry the weight of the climber. Until all these are confirmed before the climber can reliably use the ladder. Same is the case of a destiny owner, he must have a reliable ladder that can carry his weight weather to climb gently or run on it as the case maybe.

Every destiny carrier, weather prophet, pastor, businessmen and women we need destiny supports that can think more than you. I know when and what you need and are ready to support. In the case of a pastor, if you are connected to a destiny supporter, you will not need to wait for offering or contribution in the church before buying land or acquiring properties for the ministry's use. The destiny support knows you need this and will make them available.

Let me quickly tell you a story before we pray. A pastor was transferred from a branch of a church to another branch of same church in different location. So the elders at the new location refused to recognise or embrace him, though this was the handwork of the predecessor. The successor's luggage was outside for a week. When he was finally invited in for a meeting with some youth leaders and elders in attendance, they told him we understand that you are being paid N60,000 where you are being transferred from but here we are not buoyant so we can only afford to pay you N30,000. You can either take it or leave it and whatever you decide let us know. He went out and made a call to headquarters where the transfer was initiated, to report the meeting. The response he got was this,

"who called you to ministry, is it God or human that called you?"
He replied, *"it is God that called him"*, so he was told to accept
the offer that they are not transferring him to any other place.

During that meeting a young youth elder that God has
richly blessed frowned at what the elders did and regretted
attending the meeting. According to him when he met the
newly transferred pastor, who he has never met before
neither has the pastor ever prayed for him or met him
before as well. Little did he know he was about to be hit
with one of the greatest shock of his life and the man said
to him that money that you were offered you will not accept
but I personally will be paying you ₦150,000 monthly and
I will pay you two years up front immediately. There and
then he made a transfer of ₦3.6M to the pastors account
this was on a Saturday, and also said to him that I will be
paying my company's tithe to you. On Sunday morning the
pastor confidently climbed the altar. He announced that
the Lord has already spoken to him not to collect salary
from the church. His anointing began to flow, signs and
wonders were happening in the church with a large crowd
in attendance for all church services and activities. When
the elders that offered him the less amount saw what was
happening they began to plead with him and return to
his side and abandoned the predecessor. This pastor was
earning more than where he was even transferred from, he
has a lot deposited in him but he never had any support to
lean on so he will perform less or even be suffering but the
moment the destiny support for his destiny appeared, his
story changed. This Pastor's destiny has gotten a destiny
support to lean on.

7. Those that will restore you back to your throne

Many have been dethroned by the battles of their father's house. Many are no longer on the throne. Let me site an example, David was dethroned by the son whom he liked the most, who resembles him most, he is the heir to the throne and he is seen as the person that will become the next king. The son of David ganged up against his father and drove him out of the palace, and David was ruling over ordinary people. You need a person that will return you back to the throne. Many marriages have being dethroned, a strange woman has taken over some marriages, some people that you helped have taken the throne away. Some helped their superior and the throne was taken away from them. The person that took the throne from David hanged himself. This is the first person to hang himself in the Bible. Some people were raised to return the throne back for David. When throne is taken away from a person the person will begin to leave among ordinary people. When the throne is taken away from a graduate, he begins to mingle with those that did not even finished school. Those that evil battles have reduced to nothing, ordinary people, begin to wear common and cheap clothes, food, even walk meaninglessly, etc. The marriage where joy has been the order of the day before begin to be troubled all through, happiness in the morning sorrow at night, because throne has been taken from the marriage.

8. You need A Powerful Person (Men of Valour)

These can either be spiritual or physical. A great man of GOD, an anointed man of GOD, that will always use prayers to fight, support and keep you.

In Nigeria today, the great and powerful men are the likes of Daddy Adeboye, Baba Olowere, even Prophet Sam Olu-Alo is also one of them. 'Baba Abiara' ,'Baba Gideon Obiwale' ,all these 'Babas' are great and powerful men.

Now, going to secular world ,the likes of Obasanjo, Tinubu, Dangote and so on. If one has destiny and these calibres of people are present in one's life,such person would go far. Men of valour ,powerful men are those that whatever they stretch their hands to are easily gotten; even abroad. Obama is a great and powerful man. Also, the current president is a great and powerful man. One's life needs the likes of great men, and these kinds of great people can be found in *1Chronicles 12:13-40 (KJV).*

> *13 Jeremiah the tenth, Machbanai the eleventh.*
>
> *14 These were of the sons of Gad, captains of the host; one of the least was over a hundred, and the greatest over a thousand.*
>
> *15 These are the ones who went over the Jordan in the first month, when it had overflown all his banks; and they put to flight all those of the valleys, both toward the east and toward the west.*
>
> *16 And there came some of the children of Benjamin and Judah to the hideout unto David.*
>
> *17 And David went out to meet them, and answered and said unto them, "If ye have come peaceably unto me to help me, mine heart shall be knit unto you; but if ye have come to betray me to mine enemies, seeing there is no wrong in mine hands, the God of our fathers look thereon and rebuke it."*

18 Then the Spirit came upon Amasai, who was chief of the captains, and he said, "Thine are we, David, and on thy side, thou son of Jesse. Peace, peace be unto thee, and peace be to thine helpers; for thy God helpeth thee." Then David received them, and made them captains of the band.

19 And there fell away some of Manasseh to David when he came with the Philistines against Saul to battle; but they helped them not, for the lords of the Philistines, upon advisement, sent him away, saying, "He will return to his master Saul to the jeopardy of our heads."

20 As he went to Ziklag there fell to him of Manasseh: Adnah, and Jozabad, and Jediael, and Michael, and Jozabad, and Elihu, and Zillethai, captains of the thousands who were from Manasseh.

21 And they helped David against the band of the rovers; for they were all mighty men of valor, and were captains in the host.

22 For at that time day by day they came to David to help him, until it was a great host, like the host of God.

23 And these are the numbers of the armed groups ready for war, and came to David at Hebron to turn the kingdom of Saul to him, according to the word of the Lord.

24 The children of Judah who bore shield and spear were six thousand and eight hundred, ready, armed for the war.

25 Of the children of Simeon, mighty men of valor for the war, seven thousand and one hundred.

26 Of the children of Levi four thousand and six hundred.

27 And Jehoiada was the leader of the Aaronites, and with him were three thousand and seven hundred;

28 and Zadok, a young man mighty of valor, and from his father's house twenty and two captains.

29 And of the children of Benjamin, the kindred of Saul, three thousand; for hitherto the greatest part of them had kept the watch of the house of Saul.

30 And of the children of Ephraim twenty thousand and eight hundred, mighty men of valor, famous throughout the house of their fathers.

31 And of the halftribe of Manasseh eighteen thousand, who were expressed by name to come and make David king.

32 And of the children of Issachar, who were men that had understanding of the times, to know what Israel ought to do, the heads of them were two hundred; and all their brethren were at their command.

33 Of Zebulun, such as went forth to battle, expert in war with all instruments of war, fifty thousand who could keep rank; they were not of double heart.

34 And of Naphtali a thousand captains, and with them with shield and spear, thirty and seven thousand.

35 And of the Danites, expert in war, twenty and eight thousand and six hundred.

36 And of Asher, such as went forth to battle, expert in war, forty thousand.

37 And on the other side of the Jordan, of the Reubenites and the Gadites, and of the halftribe of Manasseh, with all manner of instruments of war for the battle, a hundred and twenty thousand.

38 All these men of war, who could keep rank, came with a perfect heart to Hebron to make David king over all Israel; and all the rest also of Israel were of one heart to make David king.

39 And there they were with David three days, eating and drinking, for their brethren had prepared for them.

40 Moreover those who were nigh to them, even as far as Issachar and Zebulun and Naphtali, brought bread on asses, and on camels, and on mules, and on oxen, and meat, meal, cakes of figs, and bunches of raisins, and wine, and oil, and oxen, and sheep abundantly; for there was joy in Israel.

9. Those that know the secret of the champion of your battle
It is a fact that some people are stronger than you and you are unable to bring them down despite all your efforts, you are still not able to defeat them. As a destiny carrier, you need a person that knows the secret of such people who have lived with them and know their strengths and weaknesses. This kind of people, David met them. They knew what Saul's strengths and weaknesses were. These kinds of people are mostly spiritually inclined and anointed. In the physical, they are also available. Take for instance a person in Nigeria who has committed fraud cases, the moment the story is exposed or secret licked, the antigraft agency like Economic and Financial Crimes Commission (EFCC) will be

after such a person. When sorrow, bitterness or worries sets in upon a strong man, little can they attack or trouble you.

10. Those that know where the battle or attack is coming from
Sometime ago, I followed a sister to the Eastern part of Nigeria, dressed in jeans and short sleeve shirt. My identity was not known, the lady works with a bank in Nigeria and holds a big post, so upon alighting from the vehicle, we met an old man in front of their house who inquired from her if I am the husband. He went further to tell her that none of her father's children will get married. Her sin is because her father went to school and that gave her and her siblings advantage over other member of the family. *"I repeat none of you will get married, though you all will be rich and comfortable, but getting married will never be possible"* said the man. The Baba said to me, *"you cannot marry her,"* I quickly prostrated before the Baba. Unknown to him I was playing the role of a prophet for the lady. She never believed that the Baba was the champion of her life's battle. To the glory of God, the sister got married within 6 months from that time. The Baba was down with severe stroke and could not attend any of the wedding ceremonies that took place in the same village.

I pray the secret of the champion behind the battles of your life shall be exposed, and the God of Apostle Ayo Babalola will cause their mighty downfall in Jesus name.

11. You need King Makers
Many are just moving around and many are in a marriage but are like slaves in the marriage. Your destiny needs a person that will put you on the throne. Those that will make you a king in

that company where you work, your family, in your country or locality, etc. As you are reading and some of you must have met me, I did not just get here but some people that I met before now has seen me to be a prophet, they used all they had to support my destiny, they taught me how to pray, impact great knowledge in me, these are what you would do to be great, to shine to excel, they used everything they had to support me. They made me king. They told me to pray, to stay away from these kinds of sin in order for you to get to your destination. As a woman, you are a king(leader) among the women folks in your neighbourhood, or even in Nigeria. You would have experienced how certain people are highly respected and even refereed to as *"mummy"* when in actual fact, they are still very young. Meanwhile, there are even much older women in that community that don't command such respect. As a destiny carrier, you need those king makers to elevate you to your throne.

12. Good Forecasters

As a destiny carrier, you need people that have understanding of time trends and can easily tell you what is best for you, and where is best for you. A good example is someone that has good understanding of the politics advising an aspiring politician the right party to join, that can tell you what, when, where and how. Many destiny carriers possess laudable visions but they don't have those that can make it happen around them.

13. Doubtless People

As a destiny carrier, you need people that believe in your vision, and wouldn't doubt it, no matter what happens. People that can lay down their lives for you, that is, can do anything for you. They are not the eye service type, because many destiny carriers are surrounded by people characterised with eye service. You need people that would give you their word and they will keep to it. If you are a singer and they are marketers, they wouldn't betray you neither would they let you down. This is important, because in today's world, 95 out of 100 are doubters and tricksters. If you are a child of God and a praying person, God will connect you to such great believers. Even as a prophet of God, I also need people that no matter what wouldn't doubt me. You need such people in your life, that even when you are being criticised, they wouldn't pay attention to it but they will always remember the good you have done in the past. Another thing about these kinds of people is that they don't consider your age before they deal with you, neither would they write you off because you are in the middle of trying and tough times. No is never in their character. Among my spiritual sons, there is one that the first time we met, I so believed in him. I never bothered about his present situation and he also believed in my calling. One day I gave him a thousand naira and less than 3 months from then, the man was richly blessed by God with a mighty house. The wife that brought him for prayers bought a car for him. He never doubts. This kind of people are difficult to come by these days. When you look at the likes of our fathers, Apostle Ayo Babalola, he had people that supported him and never doubted him. No matter what, Baba Babajide never doubted Apostle Babalola. He supported him till the end. Infact, history teaches us that Baba Babajide is older than Apostle, yet that was never a barrier between them. Nowadays, even the people we take as fathers in the Lord are not fully loyal to us. There are also atoms or element of doubt and reservation, this also make things difficult. If I can also get 12 loyalist that never doubt me no matter what, I am sure I will be 3 times better than where I am today.

14. Capable and Patient

Destiny carriers need patient and capable people that have what you need with them. When you are in problems, they are ready to listen and stand by you. I was in a discussion with a sister of mine residing overseas, and she said to me that there are no genuine prophet and pastors again. My response was that they still exist only that you have not come in contact with them, that is the problem you are facing.

15. Good Hearted Person / Upright

These are people that will take you to your promise land as a destiny carrier. They have one mind towards you and will see that you get there no matter what.

Note: You have to pray to come in contact with these kinds of people. Don't just read this book but you need to pray for these kinds of people to manifest in your life.

Let Us Pray

- Lord pass through my place, I want to see your presence in my life, in my business, in my family, in my ministry, in Jesus name.

- Lord that person that will bring positive and glorious change to my life, O Lord send him to me this month In Jesus name.

- Lord throughout the entire world (Nigeria, America, London, Spain) etc, the person that will bring good and positive changes to my entire life, order the person to me, In Jesus name.

- O Lord, the destiny helper that will bring big and positive change to my life, God of prophet Alo help that person. In Jesus name.

- Destiny Helper that will bring positive change to my life send him/her to me, be it pastor or prophet, God connect me with that person. In Jesus name.

- Destiny helper that will make me to encounter an uncommon breakthrough, Lord let me be connected with that person in Jesus name.

- O Lord Arise that the destiny helper (male or female) that will make me encounter an uncommon breakthrough in my father's and mother's house, in the state where I am and the world at large let me be connected with that person. In Jesus name.

- Destiny helper that will expand my territory, my work, my ministry, O Lord connect me with the helper, in Jesus name.

- Timely destiny helper that will expand my territory, Lord raise such person for me, in Jesus name.

- Call the name of Jesus, Lord pass through my side, my life, marriage, business, ministry, career. I am thirsty for your help.

- O Lord, if it my sins or my ancestor's sins that has caused my destiny to lack helpers or good things, have mercy on me.

- Call the name of Jesus, Lord push me into the hands of my destiny pathfinder and that of my destiny pathfinder to me.

- Call name of Jesus 3 times, those that will promote my destiny to the people at the top, those whose are already victorious, and have what I need, Lord push me into their hands and push them to me.

- Call the name of Jesus, those that would be ladders for my destiny to climb to the top connect my destiny with them.

- Call the name of Jesus, O Lord God, the person that will return the throne that Satan and sin has taken away from me, raise the person for me.

- O Lord God, that person that knows the secret of the champion of my battle that will end my suffering, send that person to me.

- Raise the powerful man of valour that has the very thing my life needs in his hand for me in Jesus name.

- Say Lord, the ones that will return the kingship back to me, Lord I need them, send them to me.

- Father, Son and Holy Spirit those that understand the good vision inside of me, raise for me Lord, I want them.

- Call the name of Jesus, I want the patient ones that will take me to the promise land.

- Lord I need an upright person that will support my vision and partner with me for the fulfilment of my destiny.

- Those that will carter for my need both spiritual and physical, Lord locate them for me.

- The kingship title of my glory that has being snatched away from me; Lord let it be returned to me. Those that will crown me, locate them for me in Jesus name

CHAPTER 5

What to Do to Ensure You Meet
with Your Destiny Helper

1. Accept Jesus as your Lord and Personal Saviour
When you have attained the salvation your soul, your life
will change, you will have understanding of the things of the
spirit, it might take sometime to see them manifest, but you
are secured and surely they will come.

> *3 Now ye are clean through the word which I have spoken
> unto you.*
>
> *4 Abide in me, and I in you. As the branch cannot bear fruit
> of itself, except it abide in the vine; no more can ye, except
> ye abide in me.*
>
> *John 15: 3-4 (KJV)*

Nowadays, many are praying but the result is few compared
to the intensity of prayers, being offered. Some are enjoying
the grace of the prophet, not necessarily having a personal
encounter with God. These days there are so many churches,

but miracle is few compared to the number of churches. This is so because not all abide in God. I tell my partners that it will not work when you are only interested in giving me your money, and you don't know God. It is of no benefit to me. It is better not to come close to me than to be with me and not desire to have a personal relationship with God. It is good to have salvation and it will make your helpers (angel) to stay long with you.

2. Appreciate and Value People

Never forget the help that people render to you. It is always good to appreciate them, because it is never your right, it is only a privilege, as such do not abuse it. Also, learn to value people that are around you. Many don't value their superiors at work or the person that helped them get a job, thinking it is their certificate that got them the job. Some pastors, don't value the church members hence they walk out of their lives. It is not that God is no longer with them, they just don't know the value of their people. As a destiny carrier, it is important you value and appreciate people.

3. Never Disdain People

Most often the people you rate to be nothing are the people that you need or that can help your destiny. Many churches have today lost their members due to this kind of attitude, especially in the area of supporting the less privileged in the church with prayers. Today, if you observe most of the online programmes, it is easier for pastors to see visions for people that are far away abroad, than for those at home here in Nigeria because they disdain them. The sister you as a man should have married, you disdained her because she didn't have money when you met her. The woman you are married to is not yet pregnant so you have concluded that she can't give birth to a child. Never you disdain any. I recall the testimony of a son of mine in the Lord, who was married to a pastor's daughter. He was said to have a low sperm count. As a pastor's daughter we expect her to support that brother in prayers but she refused because it is medically confirmed that the man is the one with the challenge. They used to come to the mountain for prayers before the marriage and I told him that this woman is not his wife, he replied that they have prayed over it so, I kept quiet. After a long time, the Lord revealed something to me concerning him, I had to go find him and I asked him to take his wife for a test. At that time he was unaware that she was engaged in affair with some man outside their marriage and moving her things out of the house gradually. A while after the test, she finally moved out and sent a letter to him that since his sperm cells are dead and cannot father a child, she is out of the marriage. I reminded him of the time that I told him that the Lord told me that she is not his wife, so we began praying and was also praying over honey for him for his daily consumption. For more than six months we were doing this, because the Lord wanted to further announce Himself in my ministry. I later said to him there used to be one lady that I saw him with sometime ago that he said was his sister, *"that is your wife."* He said she already has a child. I said to him that the Lord said that is your wife. He replied that he never wants to marry a woman with a child, so I replied if the Lord asked you to marry one who already had four children won't you marry her, after all the one you married without a child has left you. I asked him to go for a test and he was told that his sperm cells have now grown to 10,000 and later to multiples and he was said to now have 50-50 chances. The doctors were surprised and were asking him how did he do it. Finally, he married that woman, and in less than a month after the marriage, the wife took in and less than a year, she was pregnant with their second child. As we speak, the woman that divorced him and married another person is yet to conceive. Yesterday he was a disdained person but today, what he was rejected for, he has two of it now. Never you write anybody off.

4. You need spiritual and physical anointing

You need to have someone that is praying for you, that is supporting you with prayers, you can even hide your association with that person from the public, but you will know you have a person that is assisting you with prayers. If you recall, it was through Samuel that Saul rose to the top. Samuel prophesied into his life, the spirits of prophet came upon him, and he also became a king. You need to be anointed for exploit. Besides, you alone cannot do it, just as the Bible said in *Proverbs 27:17 (KJV),*

> *Iron sharpeneth iron; so a man sharpeneth the countenance of his friend.*

If only you can do it, then David need not have a prophet. Saul also need no prophet same for Solomon, and Abraham. These days, a lot are being brainwashed. Let me make this clear but it might not sound palatable to you, there are some battles you cannot conquer or overcome by yourself, no matter the amount of personal fasting you embark upon.

5. Prayer of victory over household battles and places of residence

If you are not a prayerful person I mean one that pray at all times, to get a destiny helper will be difficult, most especially household battles always strive to stop one from attaining breakthrough in all the things you do. With your prayers you can overcome.

6. You must be kind hearted

When you have a pure and clean heart, love for others, you will get a destiny helper. Whenever I pray for my viewers or listeners, I say to them that it is whatever I wish you that I wish myself. This show the kind of heart or feeling I have I have towards them, an indication that I don't like to see people in difficulties I always want their problem to be over.

25 But I tell you of a truth, many widows were in Israel in the days of Elias, when the heaven was shut up three years and six months, when great famine was throughout all the land;

26 But unto none of them was Elias sent, save unto Sarepta, a city of Sidon, unto a woman that was a widow. She is a kind heart person and see what happened to her.

Luke 4: 25-26 (KJV)

7. Have a Heart of Giving (Showing Mercy)

It is also very good to be a giving and helping person. I went to minister in a church in Lagos, the owner of the church showed me a lady, that she is very kind towards him and that what she does for him even his child doesn't do what she does. I said to him that when women have challenges, they tend to have a lot of men of God around them. He also replied *"she might have them, but the fact still remains she really takes care of me, she is God sent to me"*, said the owner of the church. I was moved and I said to the lady your battle is over. Some people are nice to pastors because of the current challenges they are facing. I said to the sister to buy a television set, she looked at me and she walked away. I didn't allow that to bother me. After sometime, the Baba called me that after I left he asked the lady what transpired between us and her response was *"as usual"* meaning all pastors she has being meeting are always demanding for something from her. The Baba counselled her that if Olu-Alo says to me to give him my car for a whole month I will gladly do so. So, you better go do as he instructs you quickly. But at the time I had left Lagos and back on Erio mountain so she brought the TV to Erio. Unfortunately for her, she brought the television set on a raining day, no motor bike to convey her to the mountain top. The next day I collected the Television set from her and called seven prophets. We prayed on it and I returned the TV set back to her instructing her to go gift her mother. She said to me *"I thought you are the person that want to use it"*, I replied *"if I wanted a TV set, I have people that can remove existing TV set from their apartment and give to me, even if they don't have money to buy for me."* When the lady brought the television set to her mother, she said to her *"all bloodline battle that is afflicting you through me is over today."* The mother was happy her daughter gave her the television set. In less than three months after she obeyed, men started showing marital interest in her for she was already past the age of forty. She was taking care of the mother but some battles were confronting her through her mother's bloodline, but the moment she prayed the case was settled. I picked interest in her matter because of the way she was presented to be a kind hearted person. See another biblical example of kindness, *1 Chronicles 19 :1-2 (KJV)*

> *1 Now it came to pass after this, that Nahash the king of the children of Ammon died, and his son reigned in his stead.*

> *2 And David said, "I will show kindness unto Hanun the son of Nahash, because his father showed kindness to me." And David sent messengers to comfort him concerning his father. So the servants of David came into the land of the children of Ammon to Hanun to comfort him.*

Let Us Pray

- Call the name of Jesus three times, Lord pass through my side, with the hand of power and wonders so my destiny can speak and bear fruit.

- Lord every of my sin that will stop me from seeing you or stop you from seeing me, forgive me of that sin.

- Call the name of Jesus, Father, deliver me from the hand of destiny killer that my life is stuck in his hand.

- The thing that connects or ties me with the destiny killer, Lord destroy it by fire.

- You spirit that manipulate my mind to be ignorant of my destiny helper, get out of my body in Jesus name.

- You evil spirit that always divert me from destiny helpers to destiny killers, fire of God separate me and such spirit, in Jesus name.

- O Lord use fire to separate me from destiny killers that I least expect or suspect is a destiny killer in Jesus name.

- You destiny killer in Jesus name get out of my body in Jesus name. (Speak with authority)

- Every covenant I have entered into with destiny killers; O God destroy the covenant in Jesus name

CHAPTER 6

Hindrances or Obstacles that Can Deny You of Your Destiny Helpers

I am the true vine, and my Father is the husbandman.

2 Every branch in me that beareth not fruit he taketh away: and every branch that beareth fruit, he purgeth it, that it may bring forth more fruit.

3 Now ye are clean through the word which I have spoken unto you.

4 Abide in me, and I in you. As the branch cannot bear fruit of itself, except it abide in the vine; no more can ye, except ye abide in me.

5 I am the vine, ye are the branches: He that abideth in me, and I in him, the same bringeth forth much fruit: for without me ye can do nothing.

6 If a man abide not in me, he is cast forth as a branch, and is withered; and men gather them, and cast them into the fire, and they are burned.

7 If ye abide in me, and my words abide in you, ye shall ask what ye will, and it shall be done unto you.

John 15:1-7 (KJV)

God has sent you and your destiny to be a blessing and you must produce result, but when you refuse to yield results or produce fruit or your destiny is not adding value to the people around you God is not happy with you. In *John15:1-7*, here we see that both the vine and the fruit add value to each other so God wants you to be fruitful both spiritually and physically by being a soul winner. Evangelize by preaching the gospel to unsaved souls. Physically by being a blessing to people around you. You should also be fruitful maritally, in your business, ministry etc. and when you are not you can be cut down.

For your destiny to work and be fruitful you must be ready to dwell in God. For it is when you are in Him that your destiny would produce fruits. Whether you are a prophet, evangelist, pastor, minister, congregation, individual, you cannot produce fruit until you are in Him and Him in you. It's when you are in Christ that you produce fruit. As the fruit cannot do anything without the branch and also the branch without the vine so once you are saved and you dwell in Christ you are priceless.

> **Note:** *If you are in the world you must believe either Christ or the devil in the world but living in Christ and living for Christ is the most promising and profitable one that can make your destiny to be fruitful.*

Four Things that Hinder Destiny

1. Nonchalant person or Lazy person

If you choose a nonchalant or lazy people as your company. People like this missed their destiny helpers. It's very dangerous to me associated with people of this calibre and it's dangerous if you're like that. As many that are diligent they will stand before kings not before mere man who don't have value in life *Proverb 22:29* and *Proverb 12:24.*

> **Note:** *If you have destiny and you are in the company of nonchalant and lazy people your destiny is finished. In fact your destiny is ruined.*

Your destiny can't work, move, or be fruitful if you are a nonchalant person or you are a lazy person. When people are working, hustling and you don't take a step, your destiny is truncated. In fact the Bible says in *2Thessalonian 3:10b* any soul that is unwilling to work should not eat. You chose not to learn a trade or go to school when others are doing so, your destiny is in problem.

> *The lazy man deep his hand in the pot and nothing is found in it to bring to his mouth.*
>
> **Proverb 19:24.**

If you have a nonchalant person as a husband, wife or child your home is crashed already.

2. Failure to take a steps and to fail your destiny helper when he or she tests you

You can lose your destiny helper with your ignorance.

> **Note:** *you can be tested by your helper the widow of Zarephath in 1king 17:1-end did not lose or missed her helper.*

Take a step then your helper will come to your aid to help you. There are some helpers that will not help you until you take a step and ask before you can be helped.

Matthew 7:7 the widow asked the prophet and she was giving. She didn't miss her destiny helper.

3. Destiny helper can be killed or die

The problem/battle from your Father's or Mother's house, the city where you came from, the place where you married from can kill your destiny helper if you don't pray.

Prayer: your destiny helper will not be killed in Jesus name.

Note: Anyone after your wealth can kill your destiny helper and immediately a destiny helper is killed your life is shattered and scattered and for you to have another destiny helper can take you more than seven years or more. So it is dangerous to allow your destiny helper to be killed by your enemy so that you won't enter into trouble. Pray for your destiny helper if anything happens to Him or Her your life, your destiny is in problem. Also as parents pray for your children so that at your old age your life will not be miserable if you allow the enemy to kill that child that is supposed to be the helper of destiny for the rest of the children and you as a parent.

Prayer: Death will not snatch your destiny helper in every area of your life, family, your business, your marriage, your ministry in Jesus mighty name.

4. Evil power can relocate you from where your destiny helper is

Enemy can use their remote control to relocate you from where your destiny helper is supposed to have met you and you start looking for Him or Her for years and many lose there life in the process. Many destiny helpers die before they meet the person supposed to help, many even meet them and before the day of appointment with his or her helper, he or she die or even the helper can die.

Prayer: Your destiny helper will not die before He or she helps you and even after he has helped you they will last with you.

Steps to Take in Order to Meet Your Destiny Helpers and That Will Enable Them to Last With You

There are numerous steps you can take to meet your destiny helper and from them to last with you but I will only give you six.

1. Knowing God

First of all you must know God and accept Him as your personal Lord and Saviour, this is the fastest and easiest way to be connected and locate /meet you destiny helper.

1 I am the true vine, and my Father is the husbandman.

2 Every branch in me that beareth not fruit he taketh away: and every branch that beareth fruit, he purgeth it, that it may bring forth more fruit.

3 Now ye are clean through the word which I have spoken unto you.

4 Abide in me, and I in you. As the branch cannot bear fruit of itself, except it abide in the vine; no more can ye, except ye abide in me.

5 I am the vine, ye are the branches: He that abideth in me, and I in him, the same bringeth forth much fruit: for without me ye can do nothing.

6 If a man abide not in me, he is cast forth as a branch, and is withered; and men gather them, and cast them into the fire, and they are burned.

7 If ye abide in me, and my words abide in you, ye shall ask what ye will, and it shall be done unto you.

John 15:1-7 (KJV)

The salvation of your life and soul is very important and paramount. You can't do anything without Him. In fact, you are nothing without Him and destiny is sure nothing without Him in you and you in Him. Many testimonies we heard today is not because we know Him but because He doesn't want the word of His Prophet to fall to the ground so He always established the word of His Prophet or the word spoken by His Servant. Knowing God makes you locate your destiny helpers on time and it enables them to last with you. If you are not saved, your life and destiny can lack destiny helpers for life.

2. Knowing the Value and Importance of People that Surround You.

One of the reason why many lose their destiny helper is because they are not appreciative over a little or a big thing that is been giving to them. Be appreciative of whatsoever people offer or give to you, have this in your mind that it's never your right, it's a privilege, it's an opportunity and you are just being opportune. Never take it for granted be it someone's time, money, resources, even their advice.

Appreciate your helper. Know the value of people that have helped you, because failure to do so can cause them to walk away from your life.

3. Never You Look Down, Downgrade, Underrate, or Downsize Anyone in Life.

No matter who you are, where you are today never look down on any one. Many have look down on people today and those that they have looked down on now turn to be their destiny helper in life. You might be rich today don't look down on the needy or the poor, you can have problem tomorrow and the only helper you need is that fellow you have once look down on. Know the value of your prophet, you pastor, your parents, your children, your boss, your husband, your wife etc. As a man of God know the value of your congregation.

4. Anointing can Make You Meet Your Helper.

There must be someone you can rely on praying for you somewhere for you to be connected with your destiny helper not someone deceiving you that is only after your resources.

Note: If you have a glorious future you can't pray alone, you can't pray your way out yourself you need someone with higher anointing.

Iron sharpened iron and even bible says in *Deuteronomy 32:30*, one will chase a thousand two will chased ten thousands. You need spiritual anointing and physical anointing because there are some battle that you can't fight alone in life no matter who you are.

1 Then Samuel took a vial of oil, and poured it upon his head, and kissed him, and said, Is it not because the Lord hath anointed thee to be captain over his inheritance?

2 When thou art departed from me to day, then thou shalt find two men by Rachel's sepulchre in the border of Benjamin at Zelzah; and they will say unto thee, The asses which thou wentest to seek are found: and, lo, thy father hath left the care of the asses, and sorroweth for you, saying, What shall I do for my son?

3 Then shalt thou go on forward from thence, and thou shalt come to the plain of Tabor, and there shall meet thee three men going up to God to Bethel, one carrying three kids, and another carrying three loaves of bread, and another carrying a bottle of wine:

4 And they will salute thee, and give thee two loaves of bread; which thou shalt receive of their hands.

5 After that thou shalt come to the hill of God, where is the garrison of the Philistines: and it shall come to pass, when thou art come thither to the city, that thou shalt meet a company of prophets coming down from the high place with a psaltery, and a tabret, and a pipe, and a harp, before them; and they shall prophesy:

6 And the Spirit of the Lord will come upon thee, and thou shalt prophesy with them, and shalt be turned into another man.

1Samuel 10:1-6 (KJV)

5. Prayer of Victory Over Your Father and Your Mothers House Problem.

You must be a prayer warrior and you are praying without ceasing *1 Thessalonian 5:16-18*. For you to meet your destiny helper you need to pray your way out. If you are a prayer less person you are playing with your life and destiny because the battle in your father's house, your mother's house, the family you belong to or you came from, the place where you married from will not allow you and they are ready to block you from meeting your destiny helper in life. Pray your way out.

6. You Must Possess A Good And Clean Heart.

You must have a good and clean heart to people around you.

25 But I tell you of a truth, many widows were in Israel in the days of Elias, when the heaven was shut up three years and six months, when great famine was throughout all the land;

26 But unto none of them was Elias sent, save unto Sarepta, a city of Sidon, unto a woman that was a widow.

Luke 4:25-26 (KJV)

Anybody can be sent your way treat Him or Her in a good way with clean heart. Don't be rude or bad to anyone you come across in life. Have a good heart, have a large heart, have a good conscience, have a good heart this can lead you to your destiny helper and can enable them to last with you.

7. Be a Giver.

If you are a giver you won't know when you will meet your destiny helper. Abraham and Sarah are a good example of a giver and unknowingly they met their destiny helper. They met their angel unknowingly. Don't be a stingy person it can block or deny you of meeting your destiny helper in life, know how to sow into your destiny.

Now it came to pass after this, that Nahash the king of the children of Ammon died, and his son reigned in his stead.

2 And David said, I will shew kindness unto Hanun the son of Nahash, because his father shewed kindness to me. And David sent messengers to comfort him concerning his father. So the servants of David came into the land of the children of Ammon to Hanun, to comfort him.

1 Chronicles 19:1-2 (KJV)

CHAPTER 7

Why Destiny Helpers Refuse to Help

1 I am the true vine, and my Father is the husbandman.

2 Every branch in me that beareth not fruit he taketh away: and every branch that beareth fruit, he purgeth it, that it may bring forth more fruit.

3 Now ye are clean through the word which I have spoken unto you.

4 Abide in me, and I in you. As the branch cannot bear fruit of itself, except it abide in the vine; no more can ye, except ye abide in me.

5 I am the vine, ye are the branches: He that abideth in me, and I in him, the same bringeth forth much fruit: for without me ye can do nothing.

6 If a man abide not in me, he is cast forth as a branch, and is withered; and men gather them, and cast them into the fire, and they are burned.

7 If ye abide in me, and my words abide in you, ye shall ask what ye will, and it shall be done unto you.

John 15 :1-7 (KJV)

Here Jesus is referring to destiny carriers, because you are sent for a purpose, so you are expected to bear fruit spiritually and physically and if you did not bear fruit that tree will be cut off. So for destiny to bear fruit, you must be in God. Parent make sure your children are raised in Godly manner, make them know God so that their destiny can bear fruits. The Bible said train a child in the way he should go, when he grows he shall never depart from it. It is the duty of the parents to raise a godly child. If you look at my life, I have a call of destiny upon me but it was not bearing fruit until I knew God. Only then did I begin to sprout forth with fruits, same applies to you brethren.

On my last birthday, I received lots of messages, but there was this message from some youths to me. In it was written that my life gave them reasons to surrender their lives to Christ. Without the vine the branch cannot bear fruit because they work together, so your life must be in Christ. I am inviting you to Christ, let Him dwell inside of you, then you can bear fruit. A lot of us are praying but don't know Christ. There is no way such a person can bear fruit. I said in a programme I attended not too long ago that there are some people who cannot pray and are not even friends to the devil but want to fulfil destiny. I said to them, these kinds of people are finished for they are neither here nor there. You must be on one of the two sides though one is more profitable and rewarding than the other which is Christ. Now verse 6 of the above chapter say *"If a man abide not in me, he is cast forth as a branch, and is withered; and men gather them, and cast them into the fire, and they are burned."*

It is better you be in Christ and remain in Him so as not to be cut off, gathered and cast into the fire.

Reasons People Don't Get Destiny Helpers

1. Lackadaisical Attitude

This type of people struggle to get destiny helpers because of their carefree attitude and lazy personality. Brethren, it is dangerous to be in this category of persons. A friend of mine was telling me that some of his boys listened to our online programme during lock down and they said their understanding was now enlightened that they wouldn't just attend church indiscriminately anymore because they now know some facts on how to discern the true Pastors and Prophets. However, no one would invest in a lazy person. If you are lazy forget, about fulfilling destiny. A person that has destiny to fulfil but hangs with lackadaisical attitude will have his glory fade away without knowing. If you have an idea but fall into the hands of a carefree person, your idea may never see the light of the day, we have them in ministry fold as well. One of my sons sent a writeup to me speaking about how Pastors who are Planters or General overseers will have some relief that the lockdown is over though their workers may never have been bothered cause they get their monthly pay whether the church opens for service or not. I said to him, that period is when the Planters and General Overseers are blessed because 50% -70% are never lazy spiritually, so God will take care of their needs.

You cannot be alive and not make moves toward the fulfilment of your destiny and just be saying all will be well when you refuse to make a move. These kinds of people are the type that run a company we call *"Sleep and Wake Nigeria Enterprises"* They watch movies all through the day when others are running up and down to make ends meet, they argue over football, etc. One day at Erio Mountain, I stumbled on two men arguing over Messi and Ronaldo, they were both aged 38 and 36 respectively. They were calling the footballer their children that they can even die for them. I said to them, truly they are your children but their lives are better than yours because I have been to their houses in Spain, Madrid and Portugal. I inquired from them what is their work, or trade, what qualification they have gotten, the answer was non, but here they are on the mountain praying and praying with zero trade and no qualification, what do they want God to do ? Why wont such people end up stealing, Bible in the books of **Proverbs 26:15 (KJV)** said

> *The slothful hideth his hand in his bosom; it grieveth him to bring it again to his mouth.*

If you want to know a lazy woman, go visit her house in the morning. They will not attend to open the door quickly because the whole house is littered with dirty clothes and dirty kitchen combined to give the house unpleasant odour. Some men don't like this, so they stay long outside before returning home. Also a man that has no focus too can fail as well.

2. Forfeiture of Destiny Helpers
Through little test from destiny helpers, many lose their destiny helpers. The widow of Zarephath did not forfeit her destiny helper because she had a vision, she met the prophet because

she knew he would help her. Many of you have a vision but are not ready to take steps. There some destiny helpers, if you don't ask they won't help, they will see you as if you are contempt. I have a friend, I once called him for us to pray together. I told him I am not having more than ₦2000 with me so I bought fuel in my car and we left his car and drove to Idoo Ile mountain. On getting to the mountain, someone started shouting God of Olu-Alo, God of Olu-Alo... and the noise was disturbing so I said to the person that we went to pray together that let us climb the tree top and go and pray because what brought us here is not a matter of joke. I know you are blessed with wealth but the fall of a wealthy person is not good. The man standing below the tree was crying God of Olu-Alo, am in debt help me to pay my rent. Then my friend inquired how much and he handed him two bundle wraps of ₦500 notes same as ₦1000. After the man had left, I said to him that I came here to pray because of you and I mentioned it to your hearing that I have no money on me. He replied that my Prophet you never acted as if you needed money but this man indicated that he wanted that money. That widow met her prophet so she did not forfeit her blessing.

3. Destiny helpers can die

Untimely death can take away the life of a destiny helper, so you need to always pray for your destiny helper not to die because his death can make you forfeit him. I was telling my ministry partners that if you can't pray I don't think you will be a good fit for us to work together. This is particularly important, because sometimes, the people around you are all about the financial gains and other things they can benefit from you. The day you are unable to give them these benefits, they would drop you. Hence, you must hold on to your prayer life with God who is the unchangeable changer. See, many families out there today if the rich person in the family dies, before they get back on their feet, it may take them close to 7 years or more before things begin to take shape in the family. Also some women out there were doing well while their husbands were alive but the moment he dies life never remains the same. Why? Because their Destiny helper is dead.

If your destiny helper has a challenge, it would impact you. The same applies if they die, so you just have to be praying for them. Paul the Apostle asked the church to pray for him lest he fall or the enemies strikes. Mummies, Daddies, you must be praying for your children, your spouse as your pray for yourself.

I pray for you, that your destiny helpers will not die suddenly. Those helping you in your work and business will not die a sudden death likewise mine too, in Jesus name.

4. Manipulation by forces of Darkness
This happens in a way that the power of darkness send one away from the location where one is supposed to have meet with his or her destiny helper to a place where one will just be wandering and such person may end up in partnership with the wrong person. May the mercy of the Lord speak for us.

CHAPTER 8

How to Sustain Destiny Helper

Just as we have said in the first chapter of this book that a destiny helper is someone assigned by God into your life in order to help you achieve your own destiny, it is however, surprising how some people have become a parasite in the life of their destiny helpers. They failed to develop their values and build an empire for themselves in their small space but rather are dependent solely on others who have laboured so well in building their estate to continue adding value into their uncultivated land. We live in a world that people respond to value. Nobody is willing to invest in an unprofitable deal. If you desire a lasting destiny helper, your values must be attractive, your life must have some values that attracts and sustains destiny helpers positively and those values might be your ability to give out gift, your mannerism e.t.c.

For the purpose of this study, I want us to consider the story of David and the four hundred men that came to meet him in *1Samuel 22:1-2*, scriptures says that after David had fled from

Israel into the cave of Adullam because King Saul seeks his life, four hundred men in distress, in debt and also discontented came to meet him. I believe it was the Lord who prompted those four hundred ordinary men to come and be with David which made me wonder how God will send ordinary men, men in distress, debtors and men who are discontented to David who was in great distress and was passing through a terrible situation. We would have thought that God will send lawyers, wealthy or noble men into his life. The answer is that God knows the end from the beginning, He knows what we will eventually become and knows those who suits our lives and destiny perfectly. God often times wants us to add value or contribute immensely into the lives of those who come our way and will probably become our destiny helpers.

Furthermore, the scripture says that David became their captain that is to say, he began to train them, guide them and nurture them until they became giant killers (warriors). David trained them so well that the chief among the captain called Adino was able to slay eight hundred men at once, Elenzer being one of them also slew the philistines until his hands grew weary and clave to his sword *2Samuel 23:1-13*. David had succeeded in adding value and transforming the lives of men who were once depressed and confused into giant killers.

There came a day, David longed to drink water from the well of Bethlehem which was by the gate, note David did not instruct anyone of them to get him the water because he was aware of the outcome should any of his soldiers attempt such since the well was situated right in the camp of their enemies. Well three warriors arose, broke the fence of the Philistines army and were able to fetch water for David. When they brought the water to David, he could not drink of it but poured it out to God as a sacrifice. Beloved in Christ, those warriors were ready and willing to jeopardise their lives.

Jehovah God who is the supreme being wants us to praise him with all of our heart. He wants us to offer a sacrifice of praise continually before him *Psalm 107:31*. Prayers can fail because we can liken it to a way of asking God something and it might not be answered if we ask amiss *James 4:3* but you cannot overpraise God. It is as if you are giving God his meal and when you praise God, He will give us a raise. When we praise God, He Himself comes down to inhabit our praises *Psalm 22:3*. We can imagine the gift and what God will do for whoever He is pleased with.

Beloved reader, you see that it is important to have something tangible in your hands and it is not necessarily cash but a show of love. There are several ways to add value to the lives of those we come in contact with and our destiny helpers, but for the sake of this book, I will summarise it into three categories.

Spiritual Values

Spiritual values are the need that fulfil human consciousness. The best help you can render to your destiny helper is to stand up for him/her in the place of prayers, by praying all manner of prayers for him, breaking the word of God together, give them hope when their situation looks hopeless and instill faith in them when they are fearful.

Moral Values

You can render assistance and add value to the lives of your destiny helpers by positively influencing their lives through your good conduct. Scripture says that some unbelieving men can change when they see good conduct of wives. Some people might just fall in love with your decent dressing, your ways of organisation, your speeches which are usually seasoned with grace, smiles, gift etc. to turn a new leaf and make them a better person. Your moral value which has influenced their lives positively might just be why they will do anything to help your destiny. Just to satisfy David who has added and invested so much into their lives and also contributed so much in actualising their destiny, they also never hesitated to render help to David when he needed one even without him making demands.

My beloved reader, we are in a world of values whereby majority responds to values and you need to develop your values in such a way as to attract your destiny helpers. So many people have missed their destiny helpers because of lack of character and not being spiritually sensitive to entice and identify their destiny helpers. Such people fail to identify the leakage in the lives of their helpers as in the case of Elisha in *1Kings 4:8-17*, who was able to dissect the need in the life of the shunamite woman who feeds and shelter him whenever he comes to her city. It is however note worthy that God assigns timing to everything under heaven. Therefore, some destiny helpers might be in our lives for future purposes while some are immediate helpers.

Another example is still the same David when the Amalekites invaded the city of Ziklag according to *1Samuel 30:1-31*. They went away with their wives and children and also burnt their city. They wept until they had no strength to weep anymore. The scripture says that David encouraged himself and made an enquiry from the Lord for direction and the Lord instructed him to pursue, overtake and recover all. In *verse 11* of the same chapter, David's men brought a sick man who was almost dying unto him and David and his men decided to give him a complete meal of bread, water, cake of fig and two clusters of raisins, and by virtue of what they did i.e. the help they rendered to that man, his strength was revived, life came back to his spirit and his destiny was revived. He was able to pay back the help David and his men rendered to him by leading them to the camp of the Amalekite's soldiers where David was able to recover all *(vs 19)* and there was nothing lacking to them neither small nor great, neither sons nor daughters, neither spoil nor anything that they had taken to them, David recovered all. Wow! Glory to God.

Who could have believed that the man (Egyptian man) that was sickly, whom his masters had left to die on the road was programmed at that spot by God to await David. Who could have believed that the only help needed to attract the Egyptian man was just a one time meal, not a full day, or month or year, just one meal out of the three square meal we have in a day and by that singular act of kindness, the Egyptian man was willing and able to pay or respond to the help by giving up the life of his master, his friends and the entire troops of the Amalekite soldiers including all that they have taken captives to David.

Dearly beloved, that thing that looks so small in your hands might just be enough to captivate the attention of your destiny helpers. That little show of love and kindness, that little humility and smile or the little gift in your hands as the case of the poor widow who dropped two copper coins worth only a few cents was able to catch the attention of our Lord and Saviour Jesus Christ might just be all that is required of you to get at your destiny helpers who will go out of his/her way to ensure that your own destiny materializes.

41 And Jesus sat over against the treasury, and beheld how the people cast money into the treasury: and many that were rich cast in much.

42 And there came a certain poor widow, and she threw in two mites, which make a farthing.

43 And he called unto him his disciples, and saith unto them, Verily I say unto you, That this poor widow hath cast more in, than all they which have cast into the treasury:

44 For all they did cast in of their abundance; but she of her want did cast in all that she had, even all her living.

Mark 12:41-44 (KJV)

Do not look down or talk down to anybody, not even a mad man, gate man or your maid as they also might serve as your destiny helpers at some point. When we consider the case of Naaman and his wife's maid in 2kings 5, she was able to give a wise counsel to her mistress that ended the leprosy of Naaman even when Namaan was not willing to oblige to the instruction of the prophet and was leaving angrily, she persuaded and pleaded with her boss (Naaman). At the end Naaman obeyed and was completely made whole. Always aspire to have a good relationship and if it's possible, as far as it depends on you, live at peace with all men.

> *If it be possible, as much as lieth in you, live peaceably with all men.*
>
> *Roman 12:18 (KJV)*

Physical Values

These are ways of making others feel comfortable in their bodies, homes and environment. You can help others feel comfortable when you help them meet their physical needs such as helping them with their wardrobe. A lot of people do not know how to combine the beautiful clothes in their wardrobe, you can assist them in cleaning etc. as their need be and what you are doing for them physically might be more than enough for them to help you actualize your own destiny.

Important Notes/ Prayers for Destiny Carriers when Faced with Challenges

Let us consider a man that has a destiny and need his destiny to speak, he has no one to help but he believed that his destiny must speak; See *Genesis 32: 26 (KJV)*

And he said, Let me go, for the day breaketh. And he said, I will not let thee go, except thou bless me.

From the above verse, the first thing that must be considered is the display of what we refer to as being focused. A destiny carrier must be focused, both spiritually and physically. Prophet can tell you that you are a destiny child, and you also can see signs that you are a destiny child but that is not the end. You have to work to see that it comes to pass.

Here also Jacob is seeking greatness but all the places he goes to he is enslaved and yet he is looking out for where his destiny will be fulfilled. He is searching for when he will start providing for his household, because his journey of life so far shows he is being used. You also need to ask yourself questions such as *when will I start providing for my household*. As he was going he met an angel, he said to the angel *"I will not let you go."* So while prayer can activate your destiny, if you are not focused you will not know what next. When you see the person or a thing that makes your destiny to be fulfilled, never you give up but stay put and pay the price.

> *And he said unto him, What is thy name? And he said, Jacob.*

> *And he said, Thy name shall be called no more Jacob, but Israel: for as a prince hast thou power with God and with men, and hast prevailed.*

> *Genesis 32: 27-28 (KJV)*

This man being a focused and determined man, he refused to let him go. He held on in prayer saying I will never let you go unless you bless me. He prayed, his prayer was answered.

Important Things to Note as a Destiny Carrier in Christ

- Enemies will turn you to a powerful prayer warrior and a person who can fast. In my history the challenges and the affliction that I faced made me to know God and that made me to know that God can do anything. See the life of Moses, he ran away because he was trying to fight for another man that was killed and while in the wilderness he knew God and he was empowered while he was away.

- Enemies aid the destiny carriers' sword to be sharpened :- Jacob sword was made sharpened by his enemy. Remember Jacob ran away from his brother and he knew that his brother is already well to do and he is likely to return to him so he was forced to stand up. Challenges will aid one to stand up in prayers. When you are being troubled, you will know that the next thing for you to do is pray, by so doing, your spiritual sword is being sharpened.

- Enemies make your journey to glory faster. Now if you are active and powerful in prayers, your spiritual sword is sharpened, your understanding is enlightened, then you will speed up. I tell my people that whenever you face challenges/hardship, whenever it is the toughest for you, never give up, for hardship is at the verge of ease.

Kinds of Prayers to Pray by Destiny Carriers

1. Lord show/manifest your glory in my life

2. Cover me with the beauty of your glory

3. Heart of understanding *(1 Kings 3:9 Give therefore thy servant an understanding heart to judge thy people, that I may discern between good and bad: for who is able to judge this thy so great a people?)* Let me encourage youths and upcoming men of God. I have a history so I can shine. I spent 3 months on the mountain, outside come rain come shine without going inside a building and was asking seven different things as the Lord instructed me, Power, Heart of understanding, Wisdom, etc.

My parents are church goers but not so deep, so my knowledge of God was little but I love God. I do not understand how to do it. Many destiny carriers run after the wrong things, chase what is not theirs and leaving what ought to be asked for. Growing up in my village, my grandfather speaks a lot of proverbs. One day he said to me *"a lazy man uses his backhand to choose a big portion of land and plant it, when the rain starts earnestly and the weeds are growing, he in turn uses the face of his hand to reduce or cut off most part of it and says I am tired I will work this little."* Meaning when you use your backhand to choose, it has no limit but when you use the face of your hand, you can set a limit. Those who exaggerate, promise more and deliver less, these kinds of people are not likely to have a long term sustainable breakthrough. You must have a heart of understanding. Ask for it brethren. Solomon asked for it.

4. You need two keys: They are knowledge and power. You must find knowledge and have deep knowledge of what you are doing or what you are about to do. Never be ignorant on what you do. Second is Power. Power is what makes the knowledge you have function. It can be subdivided into five types.

- Power of God.
- Power of Money
- Power of Position
- Power of Name/Fame
- Power of Connection (people you know).

5. Enlargement of your coast or territory: You must always pray for enlargement, pastor/prophet/business men pray for

God to enlarge you. In *1 Chronicles 4:10 (KJV)*,

> *And Jabez called on the God of Israel, saying, Oh that thou wouldest bless me indeed, and enlarge my coast, and that thine hand might be with me, and that thou wouldest keep me from evil, that it may not grieve me! And God granted him that which he requested.*

This man Jabez, prayed to God. You too, always pray to God to bless you with money/wealth, promotion, people that matter, enlargement of coverage. These are prayers you need to be praying.

> *I decree to you to your life power for an expansion that will scare those that surround you will come upon you in Jesus name.*

There are three kinds of Blessings that God promised in the Bible for those that have deep understanding.

1. Blessing of handwork.

2. Blessing of our children.

3. Blessing against hunger.

> *Let God arise, let his enemies be scattered: let them also that hate him flee before him.*
>
> *Psalm 68:1 (KJV)*

As a destiny carrier, another prayer that you must always pray is for God to scatter your enemies. You are surrounded by enemies, as a minister of God, a business man, even, marriage, etc all are surrounded by enemies for this destiny to be fulfilled, the enemies must be scattered and flee from your presence.

36 And it came to pass at the time of the offering of the evening sacrifice, that Elijah the prophet came near, and said, Lord God of Abraham, Isaac, and of Israel, let it be known this day that thou art God in Israel, and that I am thy servant, and that I have done all these things at thy word.

37 Hear me, O Lord, hear me, that this people may know that thou art the Lord God, and that thou hast turned their heart back again.

38 Then the fire of the Lord fell, and consumed the burnt sacrifice, and the wood, and the stones, and the dust, and licked up the water that was in the trench.

1 Kings 18:36 (KJV)

You must be able to give, sow in the life of others, offer sacrifices, make people happy. As a destiny carrier, you must be willing to pay prices and sow, those that sow in tears will harvest with joy. Giving provokes the hand of God to move mightily, and you will be amazed at what it can do for you.

One fateful day , a man of God came to the mountain to pray that he owed ₦40,000 house rent and they are about sending him out of the house, so he is on the mountain to fast for forty days. I asked him what kind of God do you serve, why will you have to fast this numbers of days to get the amount you are looking for. Besides, you are based in Lagos where to get a land of ₦1m you will have to go into a thick forest, so if you are to buy a land of 3m how many days will you have to fast?

I told him, check your life, are you the type that give? You need to ask for power, authority, and mercy over all what you are doing. If all these are in your life, other things will be easy for you. You must always adopt this for your destiny to be fulfilled.

You must call on Jesus. The blind man called on Jesus and he was saved. If you also have understanding and focus, you will be surprised at what can happen to you when you call on Jesus Christ.

Let Us Pray

(You must be aggressive, pray with holy anger)

- O Lord come through my side today, I want to see you by my side so my destiny can work.

- You arrow of destiny destroyer that is in my body out by fire in Jesus name. (Pray it 7 times with holy and aggressive anger)

- Evil eyes assigned to monitor my destiny, O God, blind their eyes in Jesus name. (Pray it 3 times)

- Spirit of my father's house ruling over my destiny catch fire in Jesus name (pray it 3 Times)

- The person I draw closer to but always harming my destiny, O God, separate us in Jesus name. (Pray it 3 times)

- Call the name of Jesus 3 times, Lord seize power from the spirit of powerful men diverting my life away from where my destiny helpers are.

- O Lord set on fire in anger every evil altar where they offer sacrifices because of my destiny.

- Lord use your fire to avenge for my destiny where they are conducting evil or bad meetings over my destiny, in Jesus name.

- Lord where they are discussing evil concerning my destiny

or conducting meetings about my destiny Lord judge them without mercy.

- O Lord every evil altar working against my destiny, pull them down in Jesus name

- O Lord arise, let all the enemies of my destiny be scattered, let them not understand themselves again (pray it 3 times)

- Call the name of Jesus 3 times, O Lord authorize the destiny enlarger assigned to me to enlarge my destiny (Pray it 3 times)

- O Lord, use (money, wealth, fame, promotion, connection and upliftment) to assist my destiny as you used it to assist Abraham and Joseph.

- Oh Lord pass through my life today; my destiny, my glory, my work, my marriage, my family, my ministry is thirsty for destiny helper.

- Lord, if it's my sin that has deprived me of victory over battles in my life and causing my destiny to lack helpers, Lord have mercy on me tonight.

- God arise push me to the hand of the helper that will lead me to the right way to the top, push the person that will lead my destiny on the right path to me in Jesus name.

- In this part of the world that I am, the helper that will

lead my destiny on the right path to the top, push me to them and push them to me. Lord help me locate them, in Jesus name.

• The helper that would show my wife the road to the top, Father push them to us, and push us to them in Jesus name.

• Father those that will connect my destiny with people that are victorious, with people at the top, with those that have something good to offer my destiny, with people that their destiny is speaking, Lord connect me with them, and connect them with me.

• Lord arise in your mighty power, the person that will connect me with people at the top, that my destiny will arise through them, Lord send them to me, and send me to them in the mighty name of Jesus.

• Father those that will connect my destiny, my wife's destiny and my Children's destiny with people at the top, connect us with those people today, and connect those people with us.

• Father those that I will rely on to get to the top, those that will be my burden bearer, Lord connect my destiny with them, and connect them with me.

• Father in this month the destiny helper that I will rely on that my destiny will rise up, that my ministry will rise up, Father push them to me, and push me to them.

- The incident that will happen that will connect me with my destiny helper and my destiny will rise from there, those that will be a pillar that will hold my destiny let me be connect with them and let them be connected with me, in Jesus mighty name amen.

- Every destiny hunter that is after your destiny will lose his or her life suddenly.

- The person that will see you without you showing yourself to him or her and will turn your life to wonder, that person that your destiny needs, will begin to search for you and will locate you in the mighty name of Jesus Christ.

- In every area of life that you have been wandering around your destiny helper will sight you in this month and you will receive the mercy and favour of God in Jesus name.

Note: You need someone that will see you and will do your destiny good, someone that will show you the way to the top.

Made in the USA
Las Vegas, NV
20 April 2021